Heidi J. Christiansen, CMA
500 Beech Street
Chaska, MN 55318

Heidi J. Christiansen, CMA
500 Beech Street
Chaska, MN 55318

Heidi J. Christiansen, CMA
500 Beech Street
Chaska, MN 55318

THE WHIPLASH HANDBOOK

ABOUT THE AUTHOR

Monique Harriton was born and educated in France. While attending La Sorbonne in Paris, she was awarded a Kellogg Foundation scholarship to study at Carleton College, Minnesota, where she received her B.A. degree. She then majored in librarianship and received a Master's degree in library science at the University of Southern California.

Since completing her library training, she has been continuously employed as a community college librarian—and is presently at Rio Hondo College, Whittier, California.

Her long-time interest in health issues, from the point of view of the consumer, led her to become an active member of the California Women's Health Network. Her articles on Whiplash have been published in both American and French magazines.

Mrs. Harriton resides with her husband in Los Angeles; they have two children. Her hobbies are reading, travel, horseback riding and cooking.

THE WHIPLASH HANDBOOK

By

MONIQUE B. HARRITON

With a Foreword by

Ruth Jackson, M. D., F. A. C. S.

CHARLES C THOMAS • PUBLISHER
Springfield • Illinois • U.S.A.

Published and Distributed Throughout the World by

CHARLES C THOMAS • PUBLISHER
2600 South First Street
Springfield, Illinois 62794-9265

ISBN 0-398-05598-X

Library of Congress Catalog Card Number: 89-4555

With THOMAS BOOKS *careful attention is given to all details of manufacturing and design. It is the Publisher's desire to present books that are satisfactory as to their physical qualities and artistic possibilities and appropriate for their particular use.* THOMAS BOOKS *will be true to those laws of quality that assure a good name and good will.*

Printed in the United States of America
SC-R-3

Library of Congress Cataloging-in-Publication Data

Harriton, Monique B.
The whiplash handbook / by Monique B. Harriton ; with a foreword by Ruth Jackson.
p. cm.
Bibliography: p.
Includes index.
ISBN 0-398-05598-X
1. Whiplash injuries. I. Title.
[DNLM: 1. Whiplash Injuries. WE 725 H323w]
RD531.H37 1989
617.1'028–dc20
DNLM/DLC
for Library of Congress

89-4555
CIP

FOREWORD

There are few injuries of the human body that are more complex than what the author terms "whiplash." Whiplash is not a diagnosis per se. It is the mechanism of injuries that result in a great variety of symptoms, clinical and x-ray findings, concerning which there is often controversies.

In this era of "high technology" and rapid transportation, in spite of the 55 m.p.h. law, and the "fasten your seat belt" laws in some states, as well as the prohibition of selling alcoholic beverages to minors, we are seeing more and more injuries of the most flexible and complicated portion of the spine—the Cervical Spine. Through the cervical spine passes the spinal cord that is a continuation of the brain. It is the trailway for the passage of impulses and blood supply to and from the central station—the brain.

Miss Harriton has written an excellent expose for the victims of neck injuries caused by the whiplash mechanism. Only someone who has had one or several neck injuries could have the understanding and the desire to help other victims by revealing to them the problems they so often do not understand. Although there are controversies concerning neck injuries, and their diagnosis and treatment, she has chosen some of the top-notch authorities to impress the readers of her book.

She has mentioned the importance of prevention of neck injuries as well as diagnosis and treatment. Each person in all walks of life should be interested in all phases of this topic. Many organizations, including government and others such as The American Association of Automotive Medicine, have been doing extensive research and promotion in this field. Also, driver education programs are imperative. All cities need to improve streets and signs and to remove all objects that impede driver's ability to avoid crashes, i.e., mail boxes, parked cars, bushes, or other objects at street intersections.

RUTH JACKSON

Heidi J. Christiansen, CMA
500 Beech Street
Chaska, MN 55318

ACKNOWLEDGMENTS

The author's thanks go especially to Ruth Jackson, M.D., F.A.C.S., for her kindness and generosity in reviewing the manuscript and for her Foreword; to Sue Precht for her illustrations; to Jane Delson for her helpful suggestions; to Edmee Danan, M.D. for her encouragement; and to Norman Harriton for his assistance with editing.

Heidi J. Christiansen, CMA
500 Beech Street
Chaska, MN 55318

CONTENTS

THE WHIPLASH HANDBOOK

Heidi J. Christiansen, CMA
500 Beech Street
Chaska, MN 55318

Chapter 1

INTRODUCTION

Within a span of 25 years, I experienced four whiplash injuries as a result of rear-end collisions. During this period I was employed continuously as a librarian, yet had never come across an article or book dealing with whiplash injuries. Curious, I did a library search but found nothing written for the general public.

Still curious, I undertook a search of the medical literature. I wanted to find out what can be done to prevent whiplash injuries, the kinds of treatment which are most effective and why whiplash injuries are associated with such a bewildering variety of disparate symptoms. Apart from satisfying my curiosity through the material gathered, I intended to write an article but wound up instead with this short book.

While doing my research, I found that the emphasis in treatment modes had shifted over the years. Earlier books recommended conservative management of whiplash injuries: they stressed the importance of rest and the avoidance of activities which could trigger a recurrence of symptoms. On the other hand, most of the books published within the last decade encourage whiplash patients to assume more responsibility for self-care, once the acute stage is over; they also recommend the wide array of modalities that sports medicine favors, including physiotherapy and exercise rather than drugs and rest.

During my search of the medical literature, I realized how fortunate I had been in receiving treatment from an osteopath of the old school who was expert in the art of gentle stretching and conservative in his use of manipulation. The "passive exercise" (massage plus heat) which I received immediately after the rear-end collisions had helped minimize the chronic stiffness associated with whiplash injuries.

THE MALINGERING CONTROVERSY

Nearly all medical authors writing about whiplash injuries warn against malingerers but although examination can detect patients whose symptoms are feigned, there have been no statistical studies of malingering. An attitude of suspicion is so pervasive among many health care providers that even those whiplash victims who have been seriously injured are placed in the frustrating position of having to defend the authenticity of their complaints.

It is reported that some doctors flatly refuse to see patients who have been injured in rear-end collisions, to avoid involvement in litigation. The fact that the whiplash patient may later seek compensation from the person responsible for the accident and injury should have no bearing on the availability of quality medical care.

Some health care providers routinely discount a whiplash victim's complaints, under the assumption that they are exaggerated at best, and that the only treatment required is the "green poultice" of financial compensation from the party at fault.

Dr. R. Cloward reminds physicians that "they should not consider the patient neurotic or a malingerer until every effort to determine the presence of an organic lesion has been exhausted both before and after litigation settlement." If Dr. Cloward's advice were universally followed by his colleagues, whiplash patients would be more likely to receive appropriate care.

Drs. J. Wickstrom and H. LaRocca point out that "the physician frequently considers the symptoms bizarre and attributes them to a desire for secondary gains. The physician who decides nothing could be wrong, because there are no x-ray findings, convinces the patient that there must be collusion between the treating physician and the insurance carrier."

Dr. J. Paterson comments that "the connection between cervical spinal problems and these often bizarre symptoms is far from fanciful; nevertheless the fact is not widely appreciated and these patients are frequently still regarded with suspicion."

There is no denying the severity of some whiplash injuries: Dr. I. MacNab believes that the physician who fails to treat a whiplash patient may be responsible for producing the so-called litigation neurosis.

Hands-on health care providers do not share the distrust of whiplash patients which is present among some medical doctors. Cranial osteopaths, for example, can detect the perturbation caused by the car accident through palpation of the skull.[1] Dr. V. Frymann's foreword to André

[1]Dr. V. Frymann is in private practice in La Jolla, California and on the teaching faculty at the College of Osteopathic Medicine of the Pacific, Pomona, California.

Hardy's *Introduction a l'Osteopathie Cranienne: le Dommage du Coup de Fouet*, Paris: Peyronnet, 1967, states: skilled examination of the skull "enables the physician and the attorney to recognize that the patient who is still complaining long after the car accident is not a malingerer, but a sick person with a physical structural problem which needs specific physical help." Dr. Frymann goes on to state that "this monograph renders a great service to victims of the whiplash injury by exposing the true nature of their malady and by indicating the way in which the physician may relieve them of their afflictions."

Why do many medical doctors question the whiplash patient's complaints, while hands-on practitioners almost always accept them as valid? Physicians depend heavily upon objective tests as diagnostic tools but, at present, many of the whiplash patients' complaints cannot be validated with generally accepted tests. Also, the great variety of complaints that trouble whiplash patients do not at first appear to add up to one clear-cut syndrome which can logically be related to the whiplash injury.

The neck is central to the function of the body and is filled with vital structures. It can cause pain and dysfunction in other parts of the body. While many dentists are aware of the causal relationship between a whiplash injury and temporomandibular joint dysfunction, some ophthalmologists, otologists or urologists may overlook the fact that their patients' blurred vision, ringing in the ears or neurogenic bladder could have been caused by a whiplash accident. Seldom will a connection be made between the complaint and a rear-end collision; in many instances, when told of an old whiplash injury, the specialist lacks the knowledge to recognize the old trauma as a possible cause of the patient's symptoms.

STATISTICS

Whiplash injuries, most of which result in soft tissue injuries, are a frequent outcome of urban automobile accidents; they usually involve a rear-end collision at low speed. According to the latest edition of *Accident Facts,* there are over 4,000,000 rear-end collisions a year in the United States; they account for more than one third of all automobile accidents. In California alone, more than 80,000 injuries caused by rear-end collisions are reported yearly to the California Highway Patrol.

Dr. Ruth Jackson, the author of *The Cervical Syndrome,* estimates that 90% of the disorders of the cervical spine are due to injury; 90% of these injuries are sprains; 85% of these sprains result from rear-end collisions, and are typical whiplash injuries. Statistics from the *National Ambulatory Medical Care Survey* illuminate the magnitude of the problem: an average of 5 million doctor visits are made yearly for neck pain.

As Dr. R. Bailey points out: whiplash injuries are probably responsible for more neck injuries than any other cause; the frequency of neck disability which results from rear-end collisions and the relatively slow and painful course of recovery highlight the fact that the outcome of neck injuries is not easy to predict.

Dr. M. Trimble suspects that about 20% of the passengers caught in rear-end collisions will have significant injuries and, of those, 60% will show some evidence of concussion.

Whereas statistics establish that whiplash injuries are a very common occurrence, Dr. R. Cailliet points out, "the mechanism of the injury is poorly understood; the symptoms that are attributed to the whiplash injury are vaguely described and the treatment is empirical at best." Because of this current state of affairs, Dr. R. Cailliet concludes the injured "end up neglected, mistreated, and even accused of deception."

MEDICAL DEFINITION

While not a medical term, "whiplash" has entered the American vernacular and is defined in the Random House *College Dictionary* as "a neck injury caused by a sudden jerking backward, forward, or backward and forward of the head as during an automobile accident."

"Whiplash" graphically describes the movement of the victim's body when the car in which the victim is riding is struck from behind by another car. The rear-end collision pushes the victim's body rapidly forward as it rests against the car seat, while the head is simultaneously snapped backward. In the second phase, the reverse takes place: the victim's head is snapped forward, while at the same time, the body is bounced upward slightly. Occasionally, there is a torque effect involving a twisting of the head and neck (Figure 1).

The neck which is rapidly snapped first backward and then forward absorbs most of the shearing stress. The impact of the rear-end collision causes the neck to extend and flex far beyond its normal range of motion with great force and speed. The result is that muscle tendons overstretch, ligaments tear, and some of the cervical vertebrae, which are normally rather precariously perched on top of one another, slip slightly forward or backward from their proper position.

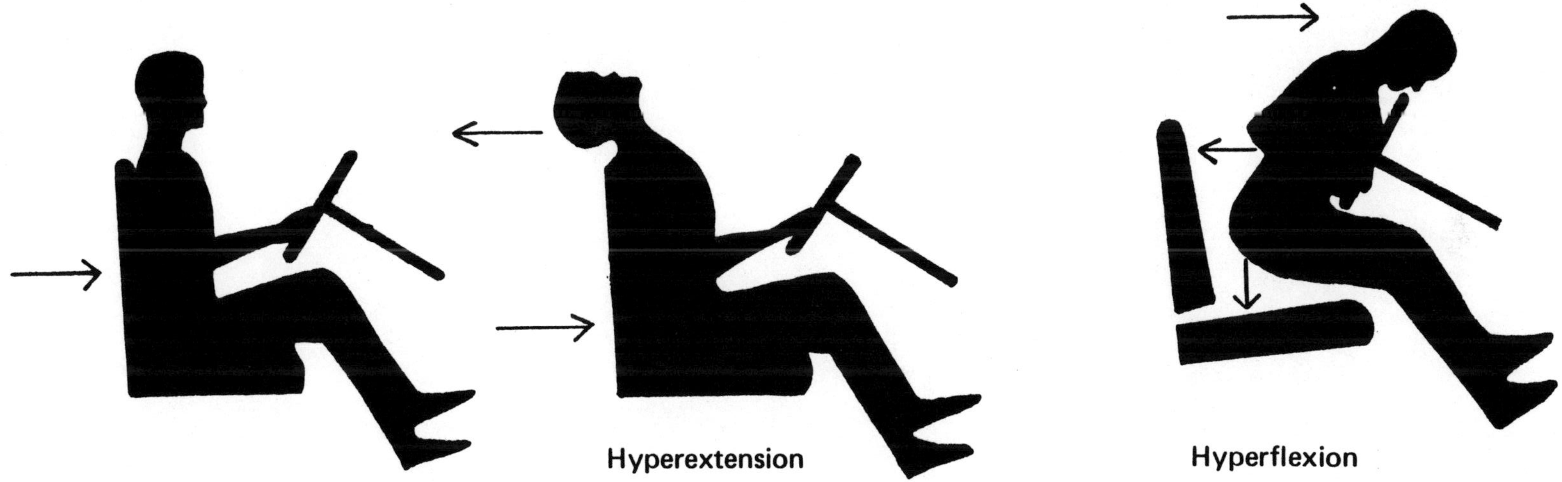

Figure 1. Rear end collision in slow motion

Although the term whiplash is a useful figure of speech describing the rapid motion back and forth that is inflicted upon the neck in a rear-end collision, the medical term for the resulting trauma is "cervical sprain [trauma to a joint plus injury to ligaments] with subluxation [displacement] of one or more vertebrae." Dr. J. Bland prefers the term "traumatic cervical syndrome" [a syndrome is a group of symptoms that characterize an abnormal condition]. Whiplash, while a medical misnomer, is a useful term which is now even used as a subject heading in *Index Medicus*, an index of medical literature. Shorthand for a syndrome, whiplash is also a springboard for controversy.

Whiplash injuries result from a complex interaction of mechanical and anatomical factors. It has therefore been found necessary to describe the laws of motion as well as the anatomy of the neck and the head in some detail, so that the nature of the injury and the complex syndrome which accompanies it, may be better understood.

There follows, not medical advice but information gathered from many different sources, which until now has not been available to the general public in a single book.

Cervical sprain
with subluxation
of one or more vertabrae
or
traumatic cervical
syndrome

Heidi J. Christiansen, CMA
500 Beech Street
Chaska, MN 55318

Chapter 2

THE REAR-END COLLISION

NEWTON'S LAWS

Dr. R. Bailey points out that **Newton's laws of motion** can help explain the mechanics of the rear-end collision which triggers the whiplash injury. Let's apply these laws of motion to a rear-end collision:

Law #1: **A body continues either at rest or in a state of motion in a straight line unless it is acted upon by an external force.** The impact of the rear-ending vehicle will exert an external force upon the rear-ended vehicle, whether it is at a standstill or moving forward.

Law #2: **The movement of a body is proportional to the magnitude of the force and the weight of the body; the body will go in the same direction as the force.** The "body" in this instance is the rear-ended vehicle; thus, if the rear-ended vehicle is at a standstill, it will be propelled forward by the force of impact; if already in motion, its speed will be accelerated. The movement of the rear-ended vehicle and of its occupants will be proportional to the weight and speed of both vehicles; the movement of the rear-ended vehicle will be lessened to the extent that the external force is absorbed by the collapse of bumpers, fenders and other structures. The acceleration of the rear-ended vehicle will jerk the victim's head and neck backward in hyperextension.

Law #3: **There is an equal and opposite reaction to every force.** The equal and opposite reaction to the forward force of the rear-ending vehicle will be exerted by the rear-ended vehicle and will be spent in decelerating the rear-ending vehicle. The rear-ended vehicle will usually be brought to an abrupt stop by a combination of circumstances: braking, wedging of the front bumper of the rear-ending vehicle under the rear bumper of the rear-ended vehicle, and collision of the rear-ended vehicle with the vehicle ahead or with some other object. In the deceleration phase, the whiplash victim's head and neck will be snapped forward in hyperflexion.

MECHANICAL FACTORS

A low speed rear-end collision may cause only minor car damage but serious bodily injury; a 10 mph collision can produce a resultant force on the head and neck of 171 pounds. Both the contact speed and weight of the two vehicles determine the severity of the impact; for instance, a streetcar traveling at 3 mph will apply as great an impact as a compact car traveling 40 mph. If the impacting car is moving at a speed 23 mph faster than the rear-ended car, this creates the environment for a severe whiplash injury. When the rear-ended vehicle is stationary at the moment of impact, the injury is usually more serious.

ANATOMICAL FACTORS

Dr. K. Winston suspects that there may be differences in individual anatomy that explain differences in vulnerability to whiplash injury. This may account for the fact that sometimes only one passenger in the rear-ended car will suffer a trauma, while others escape unscathed.

Both Dr. A. Arat and Dr. C. Goff note that the prognosis following a whiplash injury is generally good for muscular drivers; on the other hand, they believe that girls and women with long, slender necks and weak cervical muscles incur more serious injury, take longer to recover and sustain permanent disabilities more often.

Based upon their clinical observation, Drs. E. Gurdjian and L. Thomas conclude more women than men seem to be adversely affected by rear-end collisions. Drs. C. Schütt and F. Dohan carried out a statistical study which showed that "disabling neck injuries to women in auto accidents are common in metropolitan regions, varying from 6.7 to 14.5 per 1,000 women per year, half of which occur from rear-end collisions." The neck injury rate for women was 4.8 times that for men. Disability precluding a return to work averaged 8 weeks, and symptoms continued for more than 6 months in 75% of the cases. They also observed that slender women tended to have longer disability and concluded that the "higher frequency of acceleration injuries of the neck in women in contrast to men suggests that muscle strength may play a role."

Dr. M. Hohl confirmed that the incidence of recovery is better for men than for women. Dr. M. Trimble points out that about 10% of the population is particularly at risk, because of a tight vertebral canal in the cervical region, which causes the spinal cord and the emerging spinal nerves to be much more vulnerable to injury in the deceleration/hyperflexion phase. Clearly then, anatomy does play a far greater role than was formerly suspected.

According to anthropologists, the neck is a symbol of feminine beauty or of masculine strength in every culture. In proportion to the rest of the body, a woman's neck is usually longer and slimmer than a man's; not only is a man's neck usually thicker and shorter, his neck muscles are larger. The most common neck size for men is 16½ inches, while the average neck size for women is 2 or 3 inches smaller. Although attractive, a swan-like neck is a liability in a rear-end collision, while a bull-neck seems to offer better protection against serious injury.

Physical contact with the head is not necessary for a whiplash injury to occur. The brain is very vulnerable to sudden acceleration or deceleration; unconsciousness can result from deceleration or acceleration involving a change in speed of 28 feet per second, which is the equivalent of a change in speed of 19 miles per hour occurring within one second.

The many anatomical as well as mechanical variables, involved in rear-end collisions, make it impossible to determine the severity of a whiplash injury by application of a mathematical formula to the forces exerted in the collision. Validation of the whiplash injury and a determination of its severity and exact nature, can only be accomplished through clinical testing by medical personnel.

EXPERIMENTS

Experiments carried out at the UCLA Institute of Transportation and Traffic Engineering in 1966 showed the severity of whiplash injuries to be influenced by certain variables:

1. Contact speed and mass of both vehicles: these factors largely determine the extent to which the rear-ended car will be accelerated upon impact.
2. Collapse characteristics of contacting sections of the cars involved: the slight increase in collapsibility of bumpers which is found in recent car models reduces peak acceleration slightly and tends also to reduce injuries among the passengers;
3. Height and strength of the seat back: it is estimated that proper head supports should prevent whiplash injuries in approximately

half of the rear-end collisions: However, many head supports are not positioned at a height which would afford maximum protection.

4. Defensive action on the part of the potential whiplash victim: according to Drs. J. Janes and H. Hooshmand, if the whiplash victim is unaware of the impending collision and is therefore in a relaxed position, he or she is deprived of the protection afforded by contraction of the cervical paraspinal muscles, a response which usually occurs when a person is aware of an oncoming danger.
5. Physique: the height, weight, and muscular tone of the whiplash victim also play a role in determining personal vulnerability to injury.

Experiments have been considered necessary to duplicate the whiplash syndrome and to validate the complaints of whiplash patients. However, finding subjects for study, which closely approximate human vulnerability to whiplash trauma, has been a major stumbling block. Dummies were used in the experiments at the UCLA Institute of Transportation and Traffic Engineering in 1966. In the late 1970's, when the National Highway Traffic Safety Administration undertook a safety research study, it planned to use cadavers in its Biomechanics program, but the use of cadavers was ruled out by a congressional committee. The studies discussed below used primates as subjects.

A project involving rhesus monkeys was supported by the Office of Naval Research and the Naval Medical Research and Development Command. Dr. F. Unterharnscheidt reported that the combination of acceleration and deceleration can produce whiplash injuries "ranging from functional disorders to slight sprain or distortion of the cervical spine, to severe fracture dislocations with possible spinal cord involvement."

The Naval research confirmed that the flexible cervical spine can be injured in the absence of direct impact, by the sudden acceleration/deceleration of the fixed torso, which results in the hyperextension/hyperflexion of the cervical spine as the head is jerked first backward then forward. These experiments showed there is a difference between the injuries caused by hyperextension of the neck and those resulting from hyperflexion. Hyperextension can damage muscles and brain tissue, while hyperflexion can injure vertebrae, discs, ligaments, joints and nerve roots.

It was Dr. F. Unterharnscheidt's observation that the injury will be more severe if, at the moment of impact, the neck is slightly flexed in a relaxed position than if the head and the neck are held erect, braced for the crash. When the impact is such that it imparts a torque movement to the head and the neck, blood vessels, such as vertebral arteries can also be damaged and the normal blood flow to the brain obstructed. This may explain the cases of Wallenberg syndrome [characterized by muscular weakness and cerebellar dysfunction] which were seen in the experimental animals.

Study of head injuries is explicitly mandated by Congress; head injuries are considered a major national problem. The Head Injury Clinical Research Center of the University of Pennsylvania conducted a series of experiments on baboons over a 14 year period, but these were halted in 1984 when the Animal Liberation Front succeeded in having the Center's federal funding terminated. The animal liberationists exposed the cruelty with which the experiments were handled. The baboon's head was subjected to a sudden jerking motion delivered by a piston. The resulting trauma was similar to the whiplash injury that occurs in many rear-end automobile collisions. Later, the baboon's memory was tested and its brain tissues analyzed. The degree of injury to its nerve cell axons (extensions) indicated the severity of the injury. The experimenters speculated that some of the damage to the brain cells might be reversible.

According to the *Science* article which reported the break-in by the Animal Liberation Front, Dr. Murray Goldstein, Director of the National Institute of Neurological and Communicative Disorders and Strokes, which oversaw the program at the University of Pennsylvania, has concluded that "not all the accidents causing head injury can be prevented and the extent to which even minor brain injuries are treatable is very limited."

Experiments upon animals have not been publicly funded, since the abuse of baboons was exposed. How incongruous it is that when baboons are subjected to experimental whiplash injuries, the experiments are condemned as intolerable cruelty, but when human beings receive whiplash injuries in rear-end collisions, their complaints are often summarily dismissed as psychological in origin, or as malingering.

There have been so few studies of whiplash injuries that, as Dr. M. Trimble has pointed out, it is difficult to form a considered opinion. It is indeed unfortunate that humane experimental studies are not being continued, given the value of such studies in better understanding and treating whiplash injuries.

According to Dr. M. Trimble, there was one experimental study of whiplash injuries which did not utilize animals but, instead, used a lucite cranium filled with a gelatin mold of the brain. That study had arrived at many of the same findings as the primate studies did later. The transparent replica skull permitted visual examination of the effect of acceleration/deceleration forces upon the brain simultaneously with the application of those forces.

More research is badly needed to establish an official NECK INJURY CRITERION SCALE. There are two programs that collect data after automobile accidents. The *National Crash Severity Study* focuses on the engineering aspect; the *Head Injury and Spinal Cord Injury Centers* are mainly concerned with the medical aspect. The CONSENSUS WORKSHOP held in 1981 to study head and neck injury criteria recommended that an interagency collaborative program be set up between the two agencies. Its purpose would be collating and crossmatching the two kinds of data, with the goal of finding causal relationships.

Heidi J. Christiansen, CMA
500 Beech Street
Chaska, MN 55318

Chapter 3

THE NECK AND THE HEAD

A Brief Review of Anatomy

The head is a 10 to 14 pound mass; the brain itself accounts for about three pounds and its bony enclosure, the skull, for one and a half pounds. The remainder of the weight is accounted for by cartilage, muscles, teeth and blood vessels.

The BRAIN represents about 2% of the total body weight: it is about the size of a grapefruit and weighs approximately as much as a cabbage. It has the consistency of jello. It receives 20% of all the oxygen used by the body and the equivalent of half its own weight in blood every minute. One-fifth of the total blood volume in the body is found in the head at any given time.

The main function of the brain is to maintain and organize the various body processes. The 10 billion neurons in the brain monitor neurochemicals that interact to keep the health functions of the body at their optimum level. The brain used to be compared with a central telephone switchboard; more recently, the comparison with a computer has been made. However, the consensus is that brain cells are not like microchips, but are instead complex chemical interactions contained inside a saline pool, the cerebrospinal fluid which acts as a conductor.

The brain consists of the right and left hemispheres, each of which contains several parts or lobes with fairly specific functions; for instance the occipital lobes at the back of the brain are also called the visual cortex because they process visual information.

The head is supported by a spindly column, the neck, which represents about 3% of the total body weight. The neck is made up of seven small ringlike bones, called VERTEBRAE, each about two and a half inches wide and half an inch high; they are stacked on top of one another. These vertebrae articulate with each other through a well-balanced, five-point suspension system of small joints; there are 34 joints altogether in the cervical spine. The seven cervical vertebrae weigh a little less than three ounces (Figures 2 and 3).

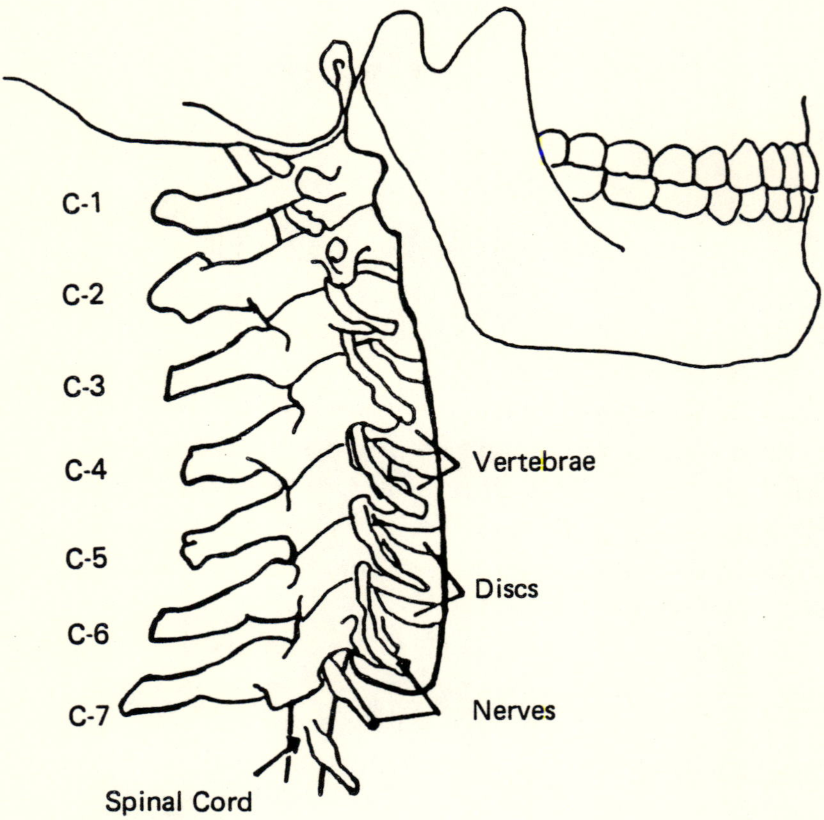

Figure 2. Cervical spine

LIGAMENTS are bands of strong fibrous tissue. There are several sets of ligaments which connect the vertebrae together, maintain them in proper alignment, and yet allow the head to turn to the sides or to bend forward and backward easily. They provide the spine with stability and strength. The ligaments have a small amount of slack and, although extensible, if stretched beyond their normal range, they can become stiff.

Cartilagenous pads called DISKS look like donuts and act as cushions between the bodies of the vertebrae. The nucleus of a disk is composed of a gelatinous substance and a network of fibers that allow for stretch and compression of the spine. In other words, disks function as shock absorbers.

The cervical vertebrae form the upper part of the spine. The spine

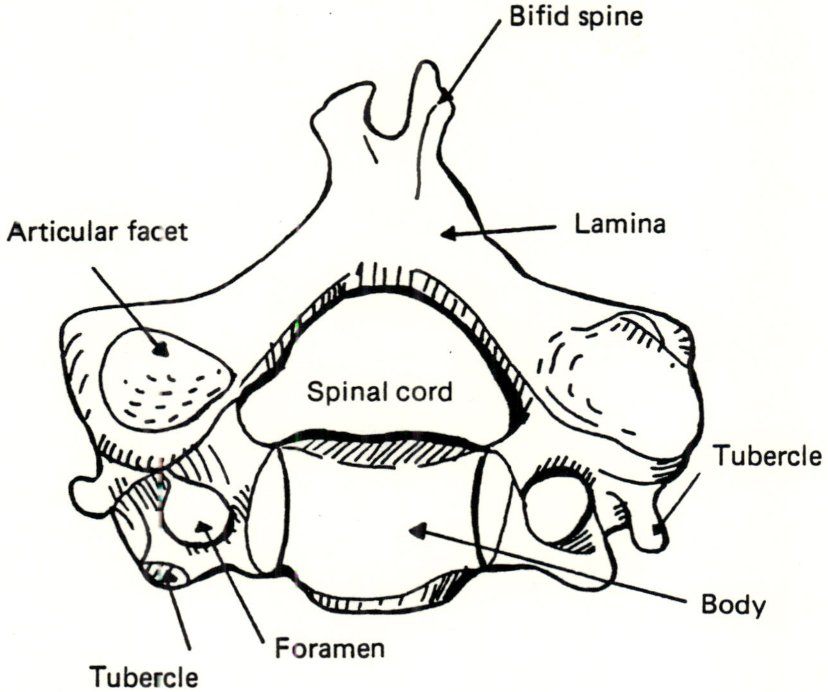

Figure 3. Cervical vertebra

which extends downward to include the tail bone, or coccyx, is commonly referred to as the "backbone." The SPINAL CANAL runs through the center openings of the vertebrae. It encloses the spinal cord which is a downward extension of the brain; there is no separation between the spinal cord and the brain.

The SKULL is the protective container which encloses the brain. It is bowl-shaped and about the size of a coconut. It is made up of eight bones that fit into one another very precisely along suture lines. According to standard medicine, they do not move. Cranial osteopaths on the other hand, claim that skull bones do move, but almost imperceptibly, at the suture lines, in a rhythm similar to that of breathing—about twelve times per minute—to accommodate fluctuations in the volume of the brain. The brain expands and contracts to maintain constant pressure of the cerebro-spinal fluid which feeds the brain and the spinal cord, and which also functions as a liquid cushion to protect the brain (Figure 4-a).

The DURA MATER is one of three membranes which line the skull and protect the brain. It also encases and protects the spinal cord, extending to the lower back.

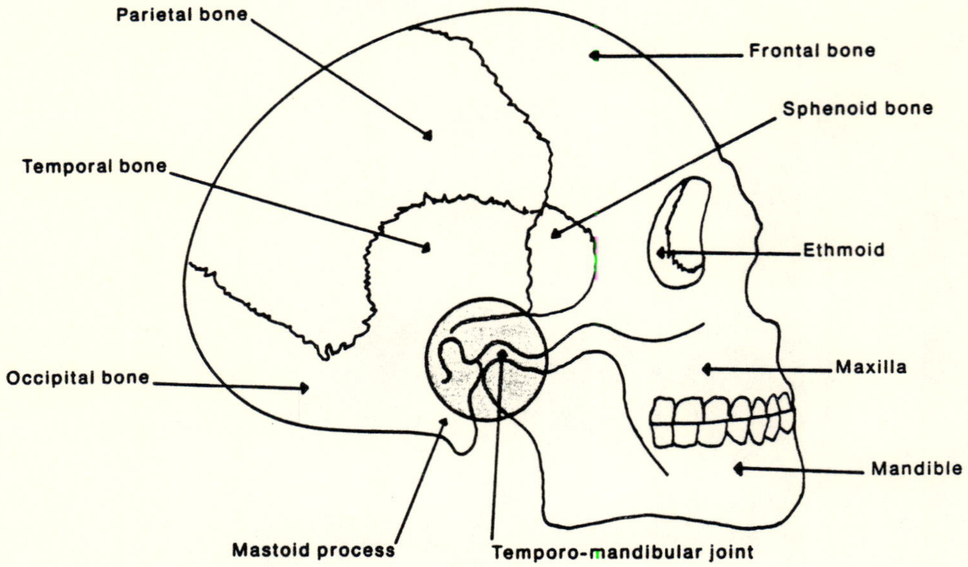

Figure 4a. Bones of the skull

Inside the skull, continuous with the spinal cord, is the BRAIN STEM, made up of a network of nerve cells and fibers; it has motor, sense and reflex functions. Before exiting through the large opening at the base of the skull, the last inch of the brain stem forms the MEDULLA OBLONGATA, which contains the stimulus centers for the heart, blood vessels and for breathing. Within the medulla oblongata is found the RETICULAR FORMATION; about the size of a little finger, it regulates the level of consciousness, from sleep to full attention (Figure 4-b).

The CEREBELLUM or "little brain" is the portion of the brain that lies inside the lowest part of the skull; it stores learned motor responses and plays an important role in coordinating voluntary muscular movements and in maintaining the sense of balance.

Next to the cerebellum and above it is found the PONS, (the bridge) which connects the cerebellum and the medulla oblongata with the upper sections of the brain. Here are found the origins of the 12 CRANIAL NERVES, sensory and motor, which govern the senses of smell, hearing, sight, and taste, as well as some of the neck muscles. Nerves to and from the trunk and the limbs pass from the spinal cord through archways between the vertebrae (intervertebral foramina). Nerves either conduct motor impulses from the brain to the muscles or they conduct sensory impulses including pain, to the brain (Figure 5).

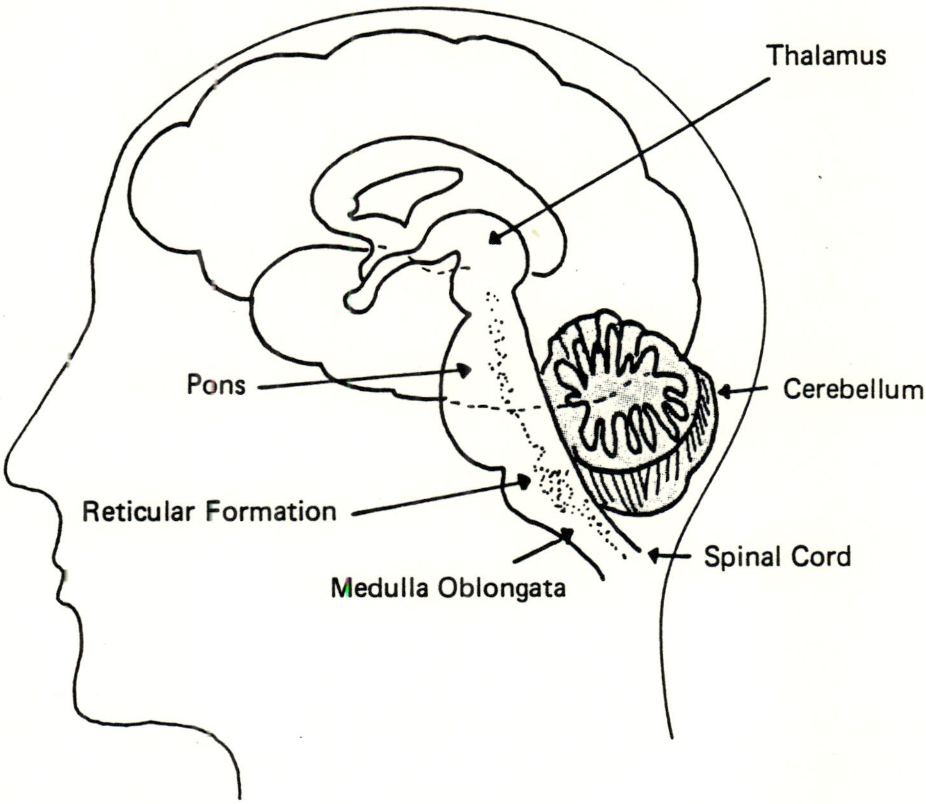

Figure 4b. Brain

In addition to the sense organs which are externally visible—ears, eyes, nose and mouth—we have another sense organ which is often overlooked, first because it is hidden from view and second because it seldom malfunctions. This sense organ is the vestibular system: located beneath the ears, within both sides of the skull, it is connected to the cerebellum. The vestibular system provides us with our sense of gravity and of balance. It helps us monitor and adjust the movements of our head and body; it also helps us detect limb position and joint angle so that, for instance, without devoting special attention to the activity, we do not stumble while walking. This sense is called PROPRIOCEPTION.

Let us now turn to the upper CERVICAL PLEXUS, which is a network made up of the first four cervical nerves in the upper part of the neck. It supplies nerve endings to the diaphragm as well as to some of the muscles that support the neck, the head and the upper back.

The BRACHIAL PLEXUS is made up of the 5th, 6th, 7th, and 8th

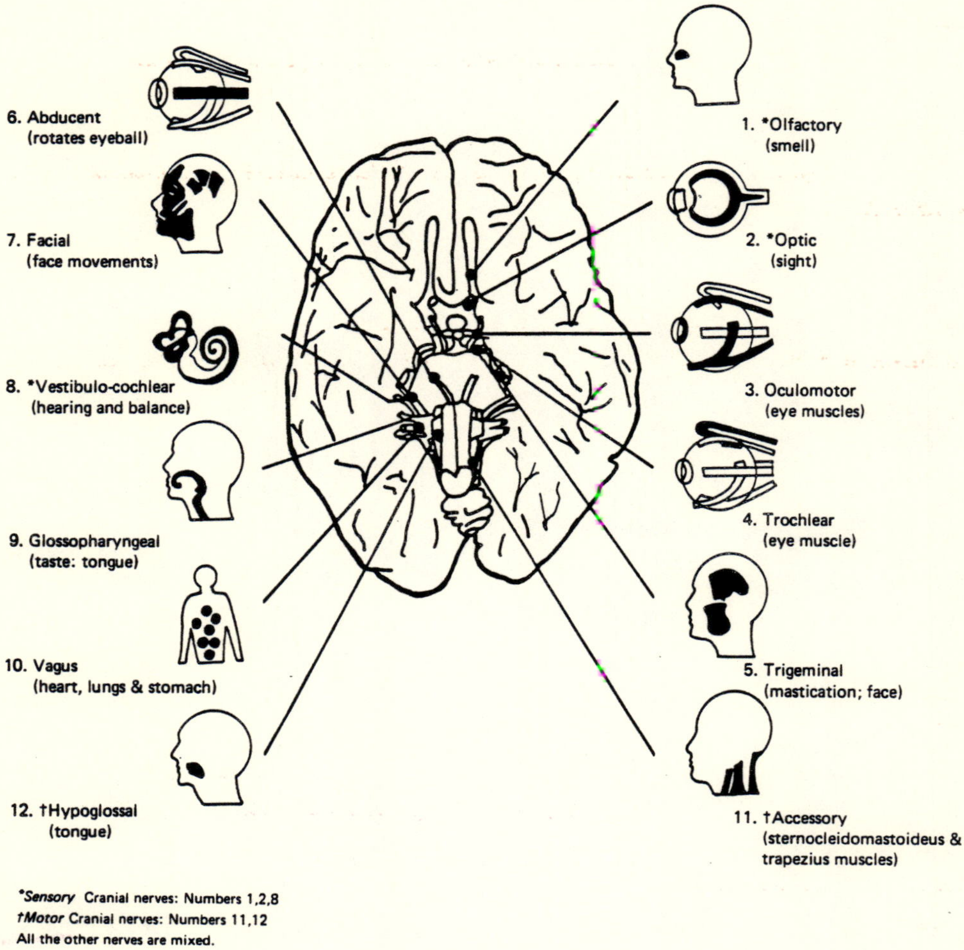

Figure 5. Cranial nerves

cervical nerves. Located in the lower part of the neck and extending to the armpit, it supplies nerve impulses to the arms and hands. It includes the median and the ulnar nerves that control the power grip and the precision grip of the hands.

The AUTONOMIC NERVOUS SYSTEM chain is located alongside the spine. In the neck region, its ganglia [nerve cell groups] are connected with the cervical plexus. The autonomous nervous system controls involuntary bodily functions such as breathing, blood pressure, heart rate, digestion and endocrine glands. It has two main branches: the SYMPATHETIC NERVOUS SYSTEM and the PARASYMPATHETIC SYSTEM. They are both active at the same time to keep functions in balance. Generally speaking, the sympathetic system speeds up body functions, while the parasympathetic system slows them down.

The sympathetic system is dominant when there is an emergency (as when, for instance, there is a need to fight or flee) and during exercise, while the parasympathetic system is dominant during rest and recuperation. The sympathetic nervous system is the thoracic-lumbar division of the autonomic system; it is activated by the neurotransmitter norepinephrine. It can speed up the heart rate and raise the blood pressure. The parasympathetic system is the cranio-sacral branch of the autonomic system and is activated by the neurotransmitter acetylcholine. It regulates the release of fluids from the digestive glands; it also controls intestinal activity and helps relax the sphincter muscles.

The main MUSCLES of the upper back and of the neck support and rotate the head sideways, flex the neck forward and extend the neck backward. Several pairs of these muscles have their origin at the seventh vertebra and their insertion at the mastoid process at the base of the skull (insertion points of muscles are movable, while points of origin are not). These muscles are the most active postural muscles of the body, as they must work steadily 16 hours a day to support the head. It is in the cervical region that extension backward and flexion forward has a wider range of motion than any other segment of the spine. Muscles, ligaments and tendons hold the spine together in about the same way guy wires hold up the mast of a ship (Figure 6). Leonardo da Vinci may have been the first to point out this mechanical analogy.

The function of the BLOOD VESSELS (arteries and veins) located in the neck is to transport blood from the heart to the head and vice versa. Especially important are the VERTEBRAL ARTERIES which carry blood to the muscles of the neck, to the spinal cord, and to the cerebellum; they pass upward at the sides of the neck through the transverse foramina (openings) of the upper six cervical vertebrae and enter the skull through the foramen magnum (Figure 7). The vertebral arteries contribute 11% of the total cerebral blood flow.

The CAROTID SHEATH should also be mentioned, because it plays a role in blood pressure fluctuations. It is located in a triangular interval between the prevertebral muscles (at the front of the neck) and the sternocleidomastoideus muscles (Figure 6) which flex the head forward and also rotate it; the carotid sheath encloses the internal carotid artery, the internal jugular vein, and the tenth cranial nerve, known as the vagus nerve. The vagus nerve has both sensory and motor functions; its

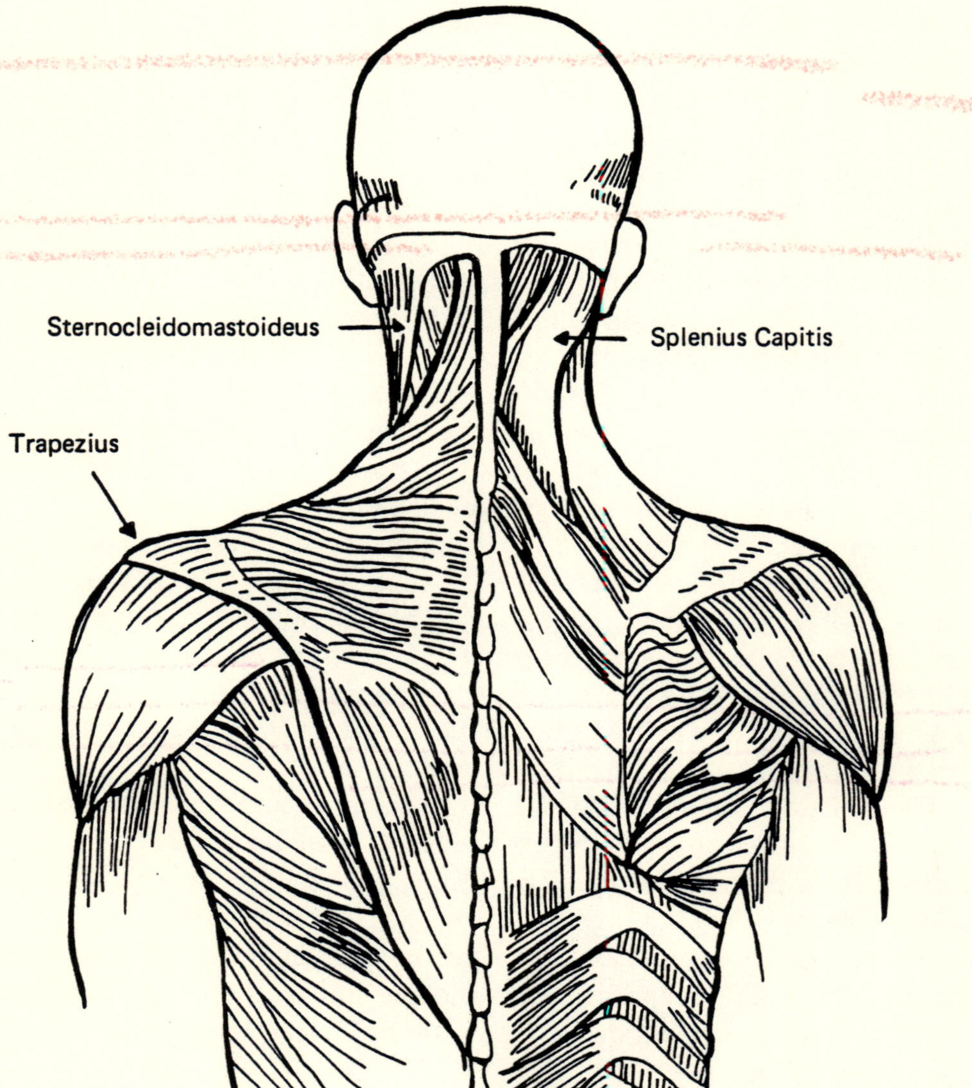

Sternocleidomastoideus & Splenius capitis *ROTATE* head
Trapezius & Splenius Capitis *EXTEND* head *BACKWARD & SIDEWAYS*
Sternocleidomastoideus *FLEX* head *FORWARD*

Figure 6. Main muscles of the upper back & the neck that are most vulnerable to whiplash injury

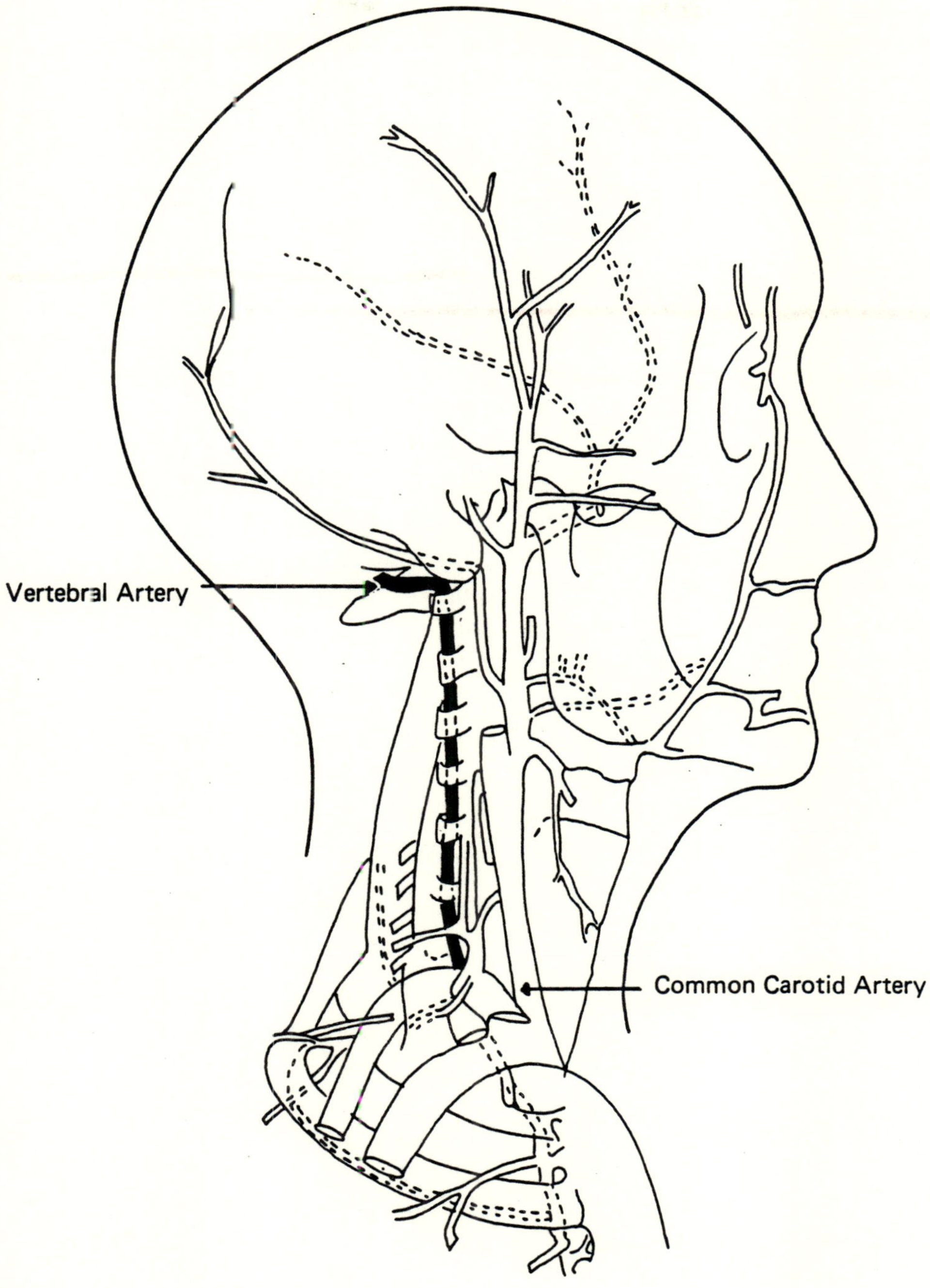

Figure 7. Main blood vessels in the neck

branches reach the throat, the heart, the lungs and the stomach: it plays an essential part in speech and in swallowing.

In Oriental medicine, the neck is called, "Pillar of Heaven"; and the acupressure points up and down the neck, "Windows in the Sky." When the neck structures are in the right alignment and the neck is not under tension, these "windows" are said to be open to the "flow of life." The neck is considered very vulnerable to tension or trauma, because there are five pairs of meridians that are located in the back of the neck, in very close proximity to one another: "Large Intestine," "Triple Warmer," "Gall Bladder," "Bladder" and "Governing Vessel." (Meridians are described in Oriental medicine as pathways where "Ch'i," the vital force in the body, circulates from one organ to another; illness or injury may disturb its flow. Meridians are not based on anatomy.)

This short overview of the anatomy of the neck will explain why it has always been looked upon as an extremely vulnerable part of the body. In oriental martial arts, it is against the rules to endanger the opponent's spine or neck. Boxing and wrestling rules throughout the world make it a foul to use the "rabbit punch," a chopping blow to the back of the neck or the base of the skull. It would appear more than a coincidence that in French, the term for whiplash injury is "coup du lapin," which translates into English as "rabbit punch."

Drs. H. Bohlman and E. Boada have pointed out that the head and the neck must be considered as one unit. Any force applied to the neck may be transmitted to the head, which explains why there is such a high association of neck and head trauma in rear-end collisions.

Chapter 4

THE WHIPLASH INJURY

There are two distinct phases to a rear-end collision. First comes the acceleration phase, in which the rear-ended vehicle receives the impact and the occupant's head is snapped **back** in HYPEREXTENSION: the point of greatest stress is between the fourth and the fifth cervical vertebrae. Next comes the deceleration phase, in which the vehicle receiving the impact comes to a sudden stop and the occupant's head is snapped **forward** in HYPERFLEXION: the most vulnerable joints are between the fifth and the sixth vertebrae (Figure 8). The fourth, fifth and sixth vertebrae are the vertebrae involved in tilting the head sideways toward the shoulders. It is therefore not surprising that whiplash patients usually find it difficult to make this movement.

According to Dr. R. Bailey, the neck bears the brunt of the rear-end collision impact because it is positioned between the rather heavy head (10 to 14 pounds) and the fairly stationary upper back and because its 6-inch length is quite flexible.

Another factor that plays an important role in whiplash injuries is the element of surprise. Drs. S. Norris and I. Watt note that the more serious injuries frequently occur when the automobile is at a full stop. The whiplash victim is usually relaxed, waiting for traffic to move, before the car in which he or she is seated is struck from behind. As the neck muscles are not contracted for the shock of the collision, there is, according to Dr. R. Cailliet, an acute stretch reflex which may result in microscopic swelling of the tissues and in hemorrhage. This in turn will force the joints of the cervical vertebrae beyond their physiological limits and put pressure on the spinal cord and on the nerves.

STRAIN OR SPRAIN

In a light rear-end collision, the injury incurred by an occupant of the car which is struck from behind is usually a STRAIN: the joints have been placed under stress by the sudden force, while ligaments and

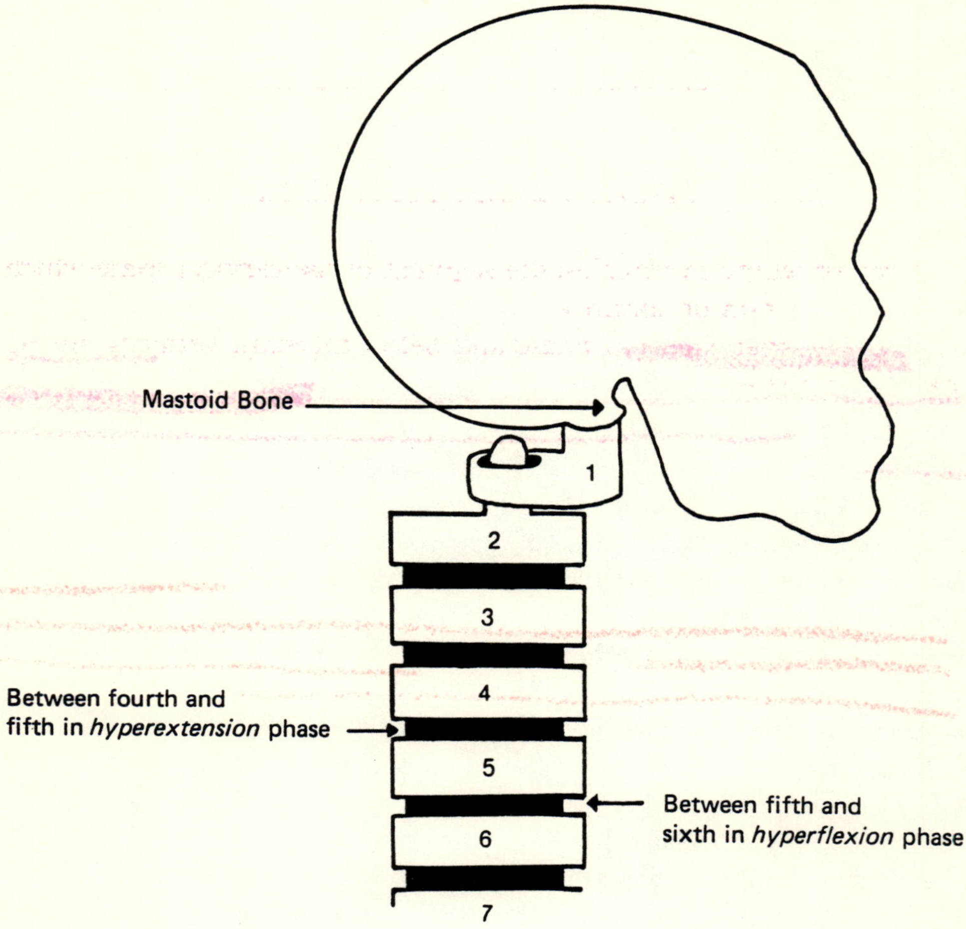

Figure 8. Points at greatest stress at the time of injury

muscles have been slightly stretched beyond their normal range. The condition will be painful for a few days but it will heal, leaving no permanent damage. In a severe collision, the injury will generally be a SPRAIN: the rending and the wrenching forces acting upon the ligaments and muscles will stretch them far beyond their functional capacity and will cause an inflammatory reaction: fluids from broken blood vessels will collect in the surrounding tissues and exert painful pressure upon nerve endings, while the bearing surfaces of the vertebral joints may be slightly dislocated.

When muscles or ligaments are injured, the pain can also spread to other muscles which were not directly affected by the injury; the latter will overcontract in order to compensate for the injured muscles which are not functioning normally. The sprains or tears of ligaments and of short muscles will heal with the formation of scar tissue, shorter and less elastic than the original tissue, thus reducing the range of comfortable motion for the affected joints. If the force of the trauma carries the vertebral joints beyond their normal range of motion, a partial dislocation or displacement of the vertebrae may result.

In repeat whiplash injuries, the segment of the cervical spine which suffers from strain or sprain will be above the fourth cervical vertebra during the hyperextension phase and below the sixth vertebra during the flexion phase.

HYPEREXTENSION of the neck can result in the compression of the cervical nerves, blood vessels and spinal cord. It can also damage the anterior part of a disk. Dr. J. Bland points out that during this first phase, even the esophagus and the larynx can both be overstretched. HYPERFLEXION can result in traction exerted upon the nerves, blood vessels and spinal cord. It can even disengage the articular processes of the vertebrae, resulting in a vertebral dislocation which in turn will cause a narrowing of the spinal canal.

The combination of rapid hyperextension and hyperflexion may also snap the spinal cord against the cervical vertebrae and could, in turn, stress the lower medulla. According to Dr. M. Trimble, for the 10% of the population who have a tight vertebral canal in the cervical region, the spinal cord could be especially at risk from being overstretched or from being compressed and this would impede the blood flow to the cerebellum.

In summary, trauma to the neck and to the cervical spine in a whiplash injury can involve:

1. Vertebrae, Disks and Ligaments:

   Subluxation [partial dislocation] of vertebrae and hair-line fractures of vertebrae.

   Laceration of intervertebral disks, which may cause pain along the border of the shoulder blade. Dr. R. Cloward points out that intervertebral disks heal much more slowly than muscles or ligaments.

   Stretching or rupture of the ligaments which hold the vertebrae in position—a very common injury.

2. Temporo-Mandibular Joint Dysfunction (involves the joint hinging the lower jaw to the upper jaw):

Common complaints associated with misalignment of this joint are facial pain, clicking noises when opening mouth, jaw held to one side, and pain while chewing. TMJ Dysfunction has become the whiplash injury of the 1980's, according to *Best's Review*, an insurance publication.

3. Muscles and Tendons:

Both sprains and strains involve overstretching and swelling of the muscles and tendons; muscles may tear if stretched beyond a certain point; the sterno-cleido-mastoid muscles are especially at risk during the acceleration/hyperextension phase. According to Dr. J. Travell, their injury is responsible for the following symptoms: dry coughing, eyelid muscle spasm, dimming of perceived light, spatial disorientation, veering toward one side, chronic sinusitis.

4. Blood Vessels:

Overstretching, compression and swelling of vertebral arteries which may interfere with free blood flow to the brain; this condition has been considered responsible for memory lapses and inability to concentrate. A possible explanation is offered by Dr. C. Fisher: vertebral arteries supply blood to those areas of the brain (hippocampus and reticular formation) which are involved in memory storage. Thus there is a valid organic basis for the mental disorganization which is common following a whiplash injury: it is caused by an impairment of the cerebral blood flow.

Dr. Y. Liu and his colleagues discovered in their experimental studies of rhesus monkeys undergoing simulated hyperextension-hyperflexion injuries that the electroencephalograms of those laboratory animals showed an unusual spiking in the hippocampus and the reticular formation; these findings would tend to corroborate the explanation for memory loss in whiplash patients which was offered by Dr. C. Fisher.

5. Nerves, Spinal Cord and Hindbrain:

Cervical nerve roots are very vulnerable to rapid compression and traction because they are quite short. A displaced vertebra may encroach upon the spinal cord. Drs. S. Norris and I. Watt point out that headaches, numbness and tingling in fingers, dizziness, and ringing in the ears are evidence of objective neurological loss.

Downward shearing and stretching forces occur within the skull during the acceleration/hyperextension phase; these forces may stress the sixth and tenth cranial nerves, (also known as the abducent and the vagus nerves) which may cause difficulties in speaking and swallowing.

6. The Autonomous Nervous System:

According to Dr. R. Cloward, the laceration of muscles in the upper back and the swelling that results from it may also irritate the adjacent sympathetic nerves and cause nausea, urine retention, or a sudden increase in blood pressure. Dr. J. Bland also blames "bizarre" symptoms such as nausea and dizziness on damage done to sympathetic fibers. Dr. R. Cailliet concurs that the symptoms that are the most confusing are those attributable to the disturbance of the sympathetic nervous system.

As bones, muscles, cervical nerves, blood vessels and the spinal cord are in such close proximity, they all impinge on one another whenever they are traumatized, creating a kind of "domino effect." It is not always possible to pinpoint the precise ligament or muscle responsible for a particular symptom; muscles and joints work together in such a way that if there is a loss of normal motion in one muscle, other joints will eventually be forced to position themselves abnormally to compensate. For instance, a forward dislocation of the 4th and 5th cervical vertebrae may cause referred pain to the front of the shoulder. The reason for this phenomenon is that there is a close continuity between the deep cervical tissues, the enveloping muscles and the nerves that penetrate the back of the head, the neck and the shoulders.

BRAIN CONCUSSION

A rear-end collision can elevate the whiplash victim's position by as much as 3 inches and then abruptly and forcibly lower the victim back into the car seat. This bouncing up and down may explain why the basal portion of the brain is one of the most common areas of injury. According to Dr. A. Arat, the hindbrain (medulla oblongata, pons and cerebellum) as well as the occipital lobes of the brain, also known as the visual cortex can be compressed against the bony base of the skull and be bruised. To quote Dr. M. Trimble, "a concussion is the direct result of mechanical violence to cerebral cells, a molecular reaction induced by physical stress," which results in an electro-physiological disturbance of the brain.

According to Dr. J. Kulowski, a brain concussion can be induced by the rotational forces that are triggered by the rear-end collision. The skull is set in motion by the initial impact; the soft brain inside the skull is displaced and bumped against the opposite side of the hard bony skull. This "contrecoup" injury occurring on the side that is opposite from the source of the impact may damage cerebral tissues. The rotation of the head will compound the injury: Drs. A. Sauces and N. Yoganandan blame rotational forces specifically for the laceration of blood vessels in the brain and for brain contusion.

The brain has been compared to a bowl of gelatin: move the bowl suddenly in one direction and the gelatin will slosh against the opposite side of the bowl. The brain does the same thing inside the hard, bony skull, injuring blood vessels and nerves in the process. It is usually assumed that direct contact is necessary for an injury to occur: this is not the case with whiplash injuries. A forceful rear-end collision can be sufficient to induce stress through rotation of the head. The brain and the skull move independently of each other, though in relation to each other, the movement of the brain lagging behind that of the skull, as Dr. M. Trimble points out.

Brain injury can be suspected whenever close observation of the whiplash victim reveals several of the following symptoms: sudden loss of memory, shortened attention span, inability to concentrate, irritability, anxiety, nausea, dizziness, disturbance in hearing or double vision. Occasionally other symptoms may be present, such as vocal cord paralysis, loss of smell or loss of taste.

SYMPTOMS

The symptoms of whiplash injury are by now familiar to many of us through personal experience. The whiplash patient is often too dazed at first to be articulate in describing his or her distress. Symptoms may appear immediately following the trauma, but they may also develop more slowly, appearing a few hours or even a few days later. Symptoms are quite varied, the only common factors being limited motion of the neck and neck pain which is aggravated by leaning the head toward the shoulders or by extending and flexing the head. Dr. R. Caillett blames neck rigidity on the irritation of the 6th and 7th cervical nerve roots. He also points out that the spot in back of the head where the neck extensor muscles attach, and where the greater occipital nerve exits, may have become very tender after the trauma.

If the neck, shoulder and upper back muscles have been sprained, there may be pain in the throat, especially while chewing and swallowing. There may also be acute discomfort in merely holding the head up, and inability to freely move the arms or shoulders and to turn the head around. If the temporomandibular joint has also been sprained, the range of motion of the jaw may be decreased.

The altered skeletal dynamics caused by the accident result in altered muscle tension which makes the patient much more uncomfortable at the end of the day. According to Dr. M. Abel, this begins a vicious cycle of skeletal and muscle imbalance. Unequal muscle tension and joint instability may cause chronic neck pain and possible spinal deformity later on.

Dr. D. Von Torklus quotes a study indicating that former whiplash patients are several times more likely to show signs of scoliosis and/or kyphosis [abnormal curve of the spine] later on in life. Drs. J. Janes and H. Hooshmand, who conducted a study of 10,000 patients with whiplash injuries at the Mayo Clinic, reported that some of these patients later developed degenerative changes such as calcification in the ligaments. Dr. W. Baxt likewise reports a high incidence of post-traumatic degenerative disease in whiplash patients. Dr. M. Hohl also states that whiplash injuries can trigger and accelerate the onset of degenerative disk disease.

Blood vessel compression may manifest itself by headaches and blurred vision following trauma of the cervical spine. Headaches are the most common complaint. An eye examination may later reveal maculopathy of the retina. Maculopathy consists of small blood clots in the retinal veins of the center spot, or macula of the retina.

Disturbance of the cerebellum, the vestibular zone of the inner ear and of the hindbrain may also cause nausea and vomiting, dizziness, loss of balance, or ringing in the ears.

The DERMATOME chart (Figure 9) shows which cervical nerves supply sensory or motor fibers to different parts of the skin and suggests which cervical nerve roots are irritated and which muscles have been weakened, based upon the symptoms which are present. For example, numbness and tingling of the fingers or weak grip of the hands is usually associated with irritation of cervical nerve roots #6, 7 and 8. Dr. M. Hinoki also reports changes in handwriting as a symptom which is occasionally noticed; presumably it is related to irritation of lower cervical nerve roots.

The whiplash patient experiences severe stress at the time of the accident. Complaints of being rattled, spaced out, stunned as if hit by a

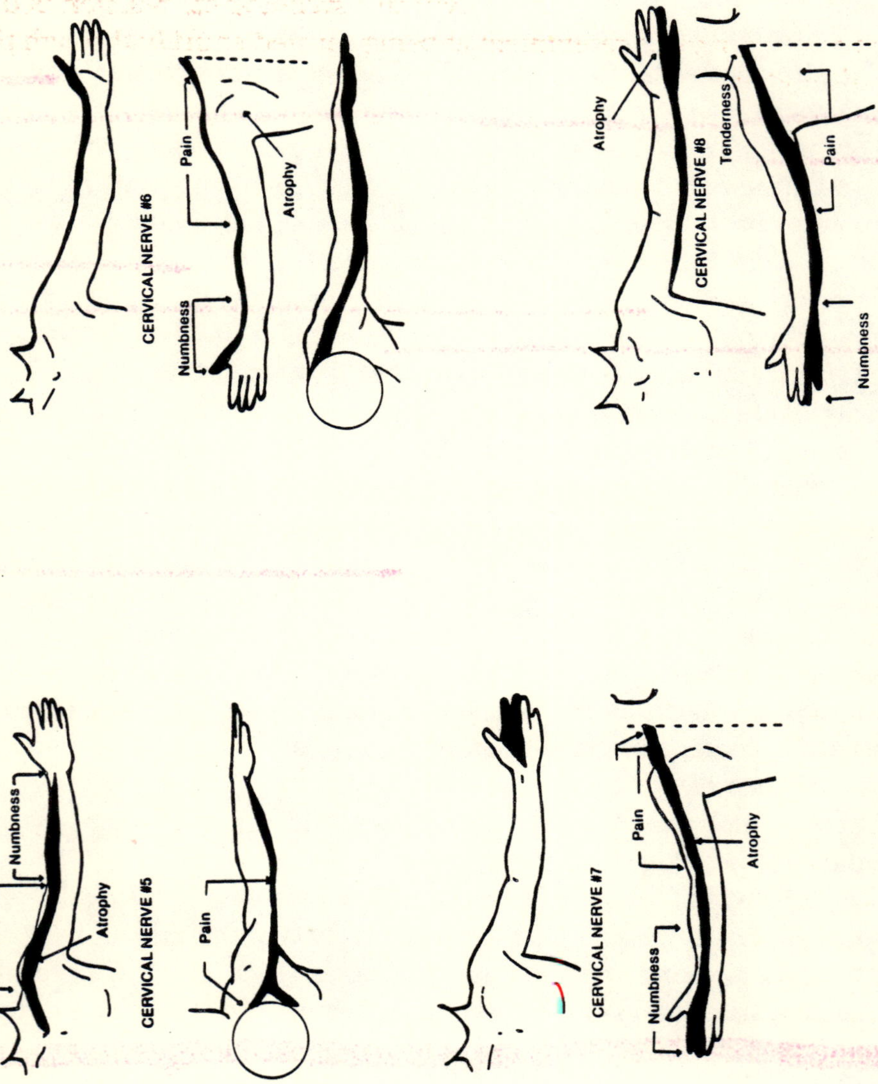

Figure 9. Dermatome chart cervical nerve root syndrome

sledgehammer, or of feeling very anxious are quite common. The fact that the accident was not caused by the whiplash victim and usually occurred behind the patient's back, without warning or with so little forewarning that there was no possibility of avoiding the collision, creates a most stressful situation: the typical psychological reaction is diffuse anxiety with great resentment at being injured entirely through the fault of another.

The medical examination given to the whiplash patient is often inadequate to reveal the nature and the extent of the injury. Upon describing the symptoms experienced, the whiplash patient is often told that "It's all in your head," or "Old age is catching up with you" or "Go home and take it easy!" The patient may even be suspected of malingering for monetary gain. In reaction to such an experience, the whiplash victim may become reluctant to mention any symptoms, other than those which are specifically related to the upper back and the neck, for fear of being branded psychologically unstable, or of losing credibility with the medical examiner.

Nowhere can the interdependence of mind and of body be better illustrated than in the case of whiplash injuries. If the health care provider ignores the interrelationship between mental and physical symptoms, correct diagnosis and optimum treatment are highly unlikely.

Emotional problems are present following a whiplash injury: crying spells and anxiety attacks are not uncommon. But the presence of such emotional problems by no means indicates that physical complaints are of psychological origin. On the contrary, it is the physical trauma of a whiplash injury that causes emotional disorders. Dr. D. Jacome suspects these psychopathological symptoms may be caused by a disturbance in the brain metabolism of two neurotransmitters.

Drs. F. Torres and S. Shapiro noted several similarities between abnormal electroencephalograms of whiplash injury patients and those of patients with closed head injuries. They concluded that neurotic symptoms usually attributed to psychological causes should instead be attributed to brain injury. They listed three possible causes: 1. The effect of acceleration/deceleration on brain tissue; 2. Injury to the brain when it hits the inner base of the skull; 3. Blood flow insufficiency produced by either constriction or partial occlusion of vertebral arteries.

Drs. C. Schutt and F. Dohan also reviewed the several reports of electroencephalogram abnormalities that occurred in a high proportion (about 50%) of humans and animals with whiplash injury. They noted that damage to the sympathetic and cerebrospinal nervous systems and rupture of the stabilizing ligaments indicate a possible organic basis for the so-called neurosis. However, another researcher, Dr. D. Jacome, was unable to confirm the research results of Drs. C. Schutt and F. Dohan, nor to concur in their conclusions.

TESTS

All patients have some subjective symptoms but subjective symptoms among whiplash patients tend to be more numerous and more varied. A medical care provider routinely attempts to confirm the presence of injury and its extent, before arriving at a diagnosis. While it is standard medical procedure to employ tests to aid in establishing a diagnosis of illness or injury, tests are not fool-proof and, even when valid, may only suggest a possible diagnosis rather than provide a conclusive one.

Dr. I. MacNab stresses how important it is to take a painstaking history of the accident, the better to properly assess the severity of the injury. He suggests the rate of acceleration to which the patient was subjected, can be estimated by obtaining answers to the following questions:

1. Weight of each vehicle?
2. Road conditions?
3. Was the rear-ended car moving or was it stopped?
4. How far forward was the rear-ended car pushed?
5. Did it collide with the car in front?
6. Did objects on the front seat land in the back?
7. Did the glove compartment door fly open?
8. Did the patient's head hit the roof? Snap back? Was it turned sideways or straight?
9. What happened to the patient's glasses, hat?
10. How high was the head rest?
11. How far back was the seat back bent by the impact?

Next, a thorough neurological examination should be conducted, during which cranial nerves are tested and reflexes checked; Romberg's test is often used to determine whether the patient can stand, feet together, while the eyes are closed, with no loss of balance. The medical care provider may also use the following tests to diagnose the extent of a whiplash injury; they are listed in order of the frequency of their use.

1. **X-rays** show bone injuries, fractures and vertebral displacement but they do not reveal the extent of soft tissue injury. Although radiology is much more sophisticated now than a few decades ago, minute bone fractures may still be hard to detect through x-rays. It is especially true of injury to vertebral joints. But, if nothing shows on x-rays, it does not necessarily follow that there has been no injury. Often a patient's complaints cannot be corroborated by x-ray findings.

2. The **Electroencephalogram** is used to record and analyze the electrical activity of the brain. After a severe whiplash with concussion-like symptoms such as loss of memory, inability to concentrate and irritability, an EEG may show an abnormal pattern of brain waves as in a closed head injury, according to Drs. F. Torres and S. Shapiro. However, the electroencephalogram is not considered a dependable indicator of brain injury resulting from a whiplash trauma, because the condition detected may have been in existence before the trauma was inflicted.

3. The **Electromyogram** measures nerve fiber **degeneration** only; if nerve root **irritation** is the problem, the results of this test will be within "normal" limits.

4. The **Electronystagmogram** detects the electrical activity of the eye muscles. A disorder in the inner ear may cause involuntary eye and eyelid movements, as well as dizziness, which is a rather common complaint of whiplash patients.

5. **Thermography** is a new diagnostic test which has elicited much interest. Thermograms are pictures of heat emitted by the body. Slight differences in tissue temperature are recorded by an electronic camera. According to Dr. C. Wexler's *Overview of Thermography,* thermography discloses areas of inflammatory nerve irritation and pain by showing them in a different color from the normal areas. However, at the time of writing, the validity of thermography remains open to question according to some orthopedic specialists.

6. Dr. M. Abel rates **CAT scans** as a superior method for "imaging the relationship between the bony structures of the spine and the soft tissue, particularly the spinal cord." This test is quite costly and is seldom used for whiplash injuries.

7. **Magnetic Resonance Imaging** (MRI) presents no radiation risks and can be better in some instances than a CAT Scan. It will produce excellent images of the soft tissues of the neck, according to Dr. R.

Martin who considers it especially valuable in diagnosing disorders of the cervical spine.

The tests described above are invaluable to the physician or to any other health care provider seeking an accurate diagnosis of the extent of the injuries; they also serve as a source of objective evidence validating a whiplash patient's complaints and symptoms.

Chapter 5

TREATMENT OPTIONS

STANDARD TREATMENT

Once fracture has been ruled out by x-rays, there are several forms of treatment which commonly are first prescribed to help relieve pain and discomfort:

1. Frequent REST periods, lying down on one's back with a small bolster-type pillow under the neck, is often prescribed (Figure 10-a). Physicians differ as to whether rest or movement is most helpful. Dr. H. Kraus states that rest does not heal but movement does; consequently he prefers using ethylchloride spray in conjunction with gentle limbering motion. Dr. J. Travell has developed a "stretch and spray" therapy technique. The full stretching of the injured muscles is made easier by application of a vapocoolant spray, Fluori-Methane (TM), which is much safer and easier to use than ethylchloride.

Dr. J. Kulowski warns that the degenerative effects of prolonged inactivity can be greater than any beneficial effect derived from bed rest. It is important to help joints through their regular range of motion. Immobilization can bring about impairment of the blood supply, edema and, later on, fibrosis as well as loss of muscle strength.

2. ICE MASSAGE over the area of pain is also often recommended; the easiest way to do this is to fill a paper cup with water, place a popsicle stick inside and freeze. When frozen, peel paper cup off the ice. Next place a cloth over the painful area to avoid frostbite. **Never** apply ice directly to the skin. Rub ice back and forth gently for a few minutes at a time several times a day. Ice applications help reduce pain and swelling, by desensitizing the affected nerve endings. The decrease in temperature causes the body to send more blood to the affected area; this increase in blood flow helps reduce inflammation and provides a continued supply of nutrients and oxygen which in turn stimulates the healing process.

3. A CERVICAL COLLAR. Dr. R. Cailliet disapproves of ready-made collars, as there are no two necks quite alike, and consequently

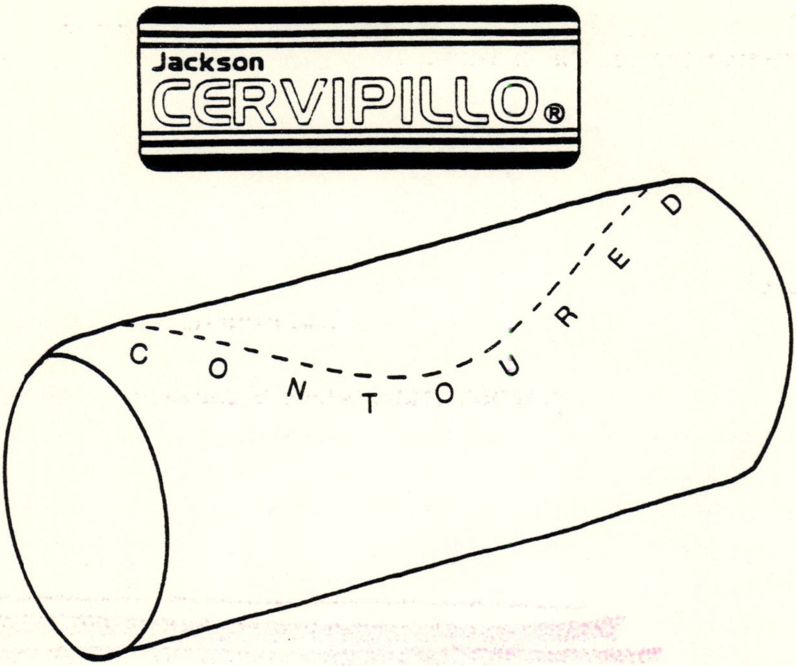

Figure 10a. Therapeutic aids

they seldom fit properly. The best collar is custom-made, higher in back, narrower in front, so that it cradles the neck in a slightly flexed position. Dr. R. Cailliet warns that a collar should not be worn continuously beyond seven to ten days; continuous use of a collar beyond that point would be counterproductive and further weaken the neck muscles. A neck collar immobilizes the injured soft tissues of the neck and helps relax them; it acts as a chin rest and helps relieve the neck muscles from strain. A cervical collar could prove especially useful in driving, as neck muscles are under particular stress, were it not for the fact that it severely restricts turning the head from side to side and would interfere with visibility.

4. MUSCLE RELAXANTS are often prescribed (one is advised against using mechanical equipment or driving a car while taking these medications). Dr. M. Hohl recommends physical measures such as rest, support and heat, rather than muscle relaxants.

TRANQUILIZERS are also frequently prescribed, even though they can exacerbate the dazed feeling which often accompanies a whiplash injury. According to Dr. H. Kraus, muscle spasm, which usually follows an acute strain or sprain, responds poorly to tranquilizers, as they are more effective for muscle tension. Dr. L. Wensel cautions repeatedly against the long term use of tranquilizers, as they can interfere with the normal functioning of the basal ganglia (nerve cell bodies lying beneath the third ventricle of the brain).

After the swelling has begun to subside, the second phase of treatment will usually consist of the following:

1. HEAT may be applied by using a heating pad which generates moist heat. (see Chapter 10: RESOURCES) Ultrasound (sound waves of low intensity which produce heat deep inside the tissues and thus promote healing) is often used by physiotherapists before massage.

2. MASSAGE by a skilled physiotherapist, chiropractor or osteopath is often administered, 2 or 3 times a week. Massage mimics the movements of exercise by squeezing and stretching the muscles. It helps increase the blood flow through the capillary vessels and the oxygenation of the blood. Massage is a form of "passive exercise." Physiotherapy and heat applications can become counterproductive, if continued beyond a several week period.

3. TRACTION is also used in treatment, preferably applied intermittently while the patient is lying on a table, with knees bent. The neck is wrapped in a heating pad which produces moist heat and the head is held in a halter connected by a cord and pulley to a weight. The amount of weight is adjustable and determines the amount of traction applied. The pull is gentle, progressive and rhythmical. Dr. R. Jackson recommends motorized, intermittent traction as the preferred form of traction. It provides a form of massage and helps break the cycle of spasm-tension-pain-spasm. Experts have concluded that traction, applied in this manner, can reduce swelling and help bring the cervical curve back to normal. It is best to keep the mouth slightly open while one is in traction to avoid excessive pull on the jaws.

Some dentists suspect that traction can put too much pressure upon the temporo-mandibular joint, (which is not a pressure-bearing joint) and that is what causes temporo-mandibular joint dysfunction. The TMJ is the articulation between the temporal bone of the skull and the lower jaw. The most common symptoms of TMJ dysfunction are: limited movements of the jaw, clicking noises at the joint and facial pain. Dr. J. Travell blames the head halter which is used during continuous neck traction in a sitting position for activating trigger points in the muscle that moves the jaw in chewing.

Dysfunction of the temporo-mandibular joint has been a "twilight" area; doctors and dentists frequently refer TMJ patients to each other. Few health care providers, with the possible exception of cranial osteopaths have any expertise in this area. Some orthodontists prescribe orthopedic splints. Physical therapists can also help with a program of postural retraining and exercises.

Traction separates the vertebrae, takes pressure off nerve roots and relaxes muscle spasms. It also helps muscles to stretch enough for the joint surfaces to glide back into their normal alignment. (Vertebrae are classified as gliding joints.) Traction does not stretch joints as effectively as manipulation, but as the spinal cord, the hindbrain and the cervical vertebrae are in such close proximity, traction is usually considered safer than manipulation in the treatment of whiplash.

4. MANIPULATION of the vertebrae of the neck, as many whiplash patients will attest, is capable of providing remarkably fast relief from muscle spasm and pain when it is administered following a series of treatments incorporating heat, massage and traction. Dr. L. Friedmann, Medical Director of the Institute for the Crippled and Disabled, Research and Rehabilitation Center, New York City, recommends that if manipulation is used, it be performed by either a physician who is a member of the North American Academy of Manipulative Medicine or by an osteopath (see RESOURCES chapter). Both professions have been trained to know when it is safe to manipulate. Before manipulation can be effectively and safely performed, the body must be prepared for it through proper physiotherapy. Manipulation could become counterproductive, if performed repeatedly.

Chiropractors focus upon the key role played by the spine in the functioning of the body and upon the importance of good vertebral alignment. In their view, the whiplash injury disrupts the arrangement of the vertebrae and in consequence the functioning of the spinal nerves. Hence their treatment stresses vertebral manipulation or adjustment to ease the vertebrae back into normal alignment.

According to Dr. L. Friedmann's definition, manipulation "stretches surrounding tissues sufficiently to unlock a joint that suffered a traumatic subluxation or dislocation and to permit the joint surfaces to be restored to their previous and normal relationship." Subluxation is the partial separation of joint surfaces; dislocation is the separation of a joint that is accompanied by the tearing of joint capsules (capsules are sheaths that enclose the point of junction between two bones). Both subluxation and dislocation usually result from the abnormal stretching of the ligaments caused by a sudden acute injury, as in whiplash injury.

Not until several weeks after a manipulation treatment do the body structures gradually contract into their former normal position. Dr. L. Friedmann cautions that the patient should not interfere with this healing process; movement should be restricted and exercise postponed following manipulation. If the patient does not allow the body structures sufficient time to resume their normal length, another subluxation may result, creating a need for further manipulation.

What is the best position for the patient to take while receiving manipulation: lying down or sitting up? There does not seem to be a consensus at the present time. Do most health care providers treat as they have been taught? Or do they perform manipulation in the position which is most comfortable to them? When manipulation is administered while the whiplash patient is in a sitting position, the treatment can be quite unpleasant and reminiscent of the whiplash injury itself. On the other hand, when the patient is on a backswing machine in an inverted position, with head toward the floor and feet toward the ceiling, the therapist can either apply gentle traction to the neck or manipulate the neck and help decompress the cervical region. In an inverted position, the body is much more relaxed and the discomfort minimal. Manipulation while the patient is upside down on the backswing machine is part of the treatment method used at Dr. R. Martin's Back and Joint Clinic in Pasadena, California; it is called **"Decompression-Mobilization Therapy"** (TM).

Many of the treatment modalities listed above have been used for many years in sports medicine. By taking full advantage of all treatment options following injury, athletes have in many cases been able to recover and return to normal form more quickly than would otherwise have been possible.

TREATMENT ALTERNATIVES

There are some other methods of treatment which are of interest. Dr. L. Friedmann, for instance, highly recommends CONNECTIVE TISSUE MASSAGE in the treatment of muscle spasms. This type of massage originated in Germany about half a century ago and is called BINDEGEWEBMASSAGE in German.

Connective tissue is widely distributed throughout the body: it surrounds or supports muscles, blood vessels and nerves. Massage of the connective tissue reportedly stimulates the parasympathetic nervous system, thus counteracting the action of the sympathetic system and helping the body "cool down."

Another option is NAPRAPATHY. The Chicago National College of Naprapathy defines naprapathy as a "gentle stretchment" of connective tissues of the spine and the joints of the body. Whereas the main focus of osteopathy and chiropractic is bone alignment, naprapathy zeroes in on ligaments (which are bands of strong connective fibrous tissue binding articular ends of bones together). (See RESOURCES chapter.)

In normal tissues, there is free circulation of blood and lymph and free movement within the nerve pathways; in addition, all the muscles, joint tendons and ligaments also move freely. Trauma interferes with free motion and results in congestion and inflammation. The purpose of naprapathic manipulation is to overcome this stalling of body function and to restore freedom of flow and movement. Connective body massage and naprapathy may not be readily available in some parts of the country.

CRANIAL OSTEOPATHY aims at 1) stabilizing the alignment of the bones of the skull and 2) bringing back the normal rhythmical cycle of "brain breathing." According to cranial osteopaths, a whiplash injury may 1) overstretch the dura mater, the outer membrane which protects the brain and the spinal cord and maintains the 8 skull bones in normal position; 2) disrupt the proper alignment of the skullbones, which are finely beveled, notched and angled, so that they interface precisely with one another. These skull bones move ever so slightly to accommodate the fluctuation of the brain tissues according to a rhythmical cycle of contraction and expansion, at the rate of about 12 times per minute; and 3) disturb the normal flow of the cerebro-spinal fluid which acts as a buffer and protects the brain from compression. Cranial osteopaths are able to detect any minute changes in the skull, and through manual therapy are able to help restore this complex cranial mechanism to normalcy. Cranial osteopaths do not use mechanically applied traction, only manual traction (see RESOURCES chapter).

HOMEOPATHY can also help. According to Dr. M. Blackie, physician to the royal family of England, head injuries frequently respond very well to homeopathic treatment. NATRUM SULPHURICUM is considered as one of the best after-injury remedies; it is especially good for the relief of symptoms of head trauma (headaches, behavioral changes, depression and difficulty in concentration). A homeopathic treatment should be preceded by a complete medical and neurological examination (see RESOURCES chapter).

BODY WORK therapies such as the Feldenkrais method or Rolfing are also of interest: the FELDENKRAIS method teaches the patient slow, gentle exercises. The goal is to change faulty neurological patterns through conscious movement retraining. This is a sensory-motor approach that is designed to "program" the brain by means of prescribed exercises, a form of motor patterning. Feldenkrais exercises are usually done while lying down to minimize the pull of gravity (see RESOURCES chapter).

ROLFING is an intense, sometimes painful, form of body reshaping that is usually accomplished by the Rolfer therapist in a series of ten sessions. The aim is to improve body alignment by loosening muscle fasciae (connective tissues) and repositioning body segments (see RESOURCES chapter). The ideal, structurally well-organized, or integrated human being has an efficient, graceful relationship to the field of gravity: the body shows a weight transmission that remains close to a vertical central axis from the center of the ear down to the shoulder, hip, knee and ankle. In the course of life, physical accidents such as whiplash injuries or bad postural habits produce muscle imbalances and misalignments, which the Rolfer therapist seeks to correct.

EXERCISES AND SPORTS

In an effort to avoid pain and recover from shock, the whiplash patient is at rest to such an extent that joints stiffen and there is a loss of muscle tone and bone mass. It is therefore important for the whiplash patient to regain a more normal range of motion through stretching and rotating exercises; such exercises are to be done slowly and gently, either after applying heat or while under a hot shower. (There is a good list of exercises given in *The Care of the Neck* by Drs. W. K. Ishmael and H. B. Shorbe (Lippincott, 1966) (see also EXERCISES chapter).

The inverted position on the backswing machine may make stretching and rotation exercises easier to do. The backswing machine should always be used on an empty stomach and for no more than three to five minutes at a time. As the inverted position is suspected of creating increased pressure both in the eyes and in the brain, the advisibility of its use should first be discussed with one's health care provider (see Figures 10b, 11a and 11b). It is said that Hippocrates himself tied patients suffering from a backache on a rack and then turned it upside down to provide relief. The backswing machine is actually a modern version of a rope trapeze apparatus that was devised years ago by the yoga master, B. K. S. Iyengar.

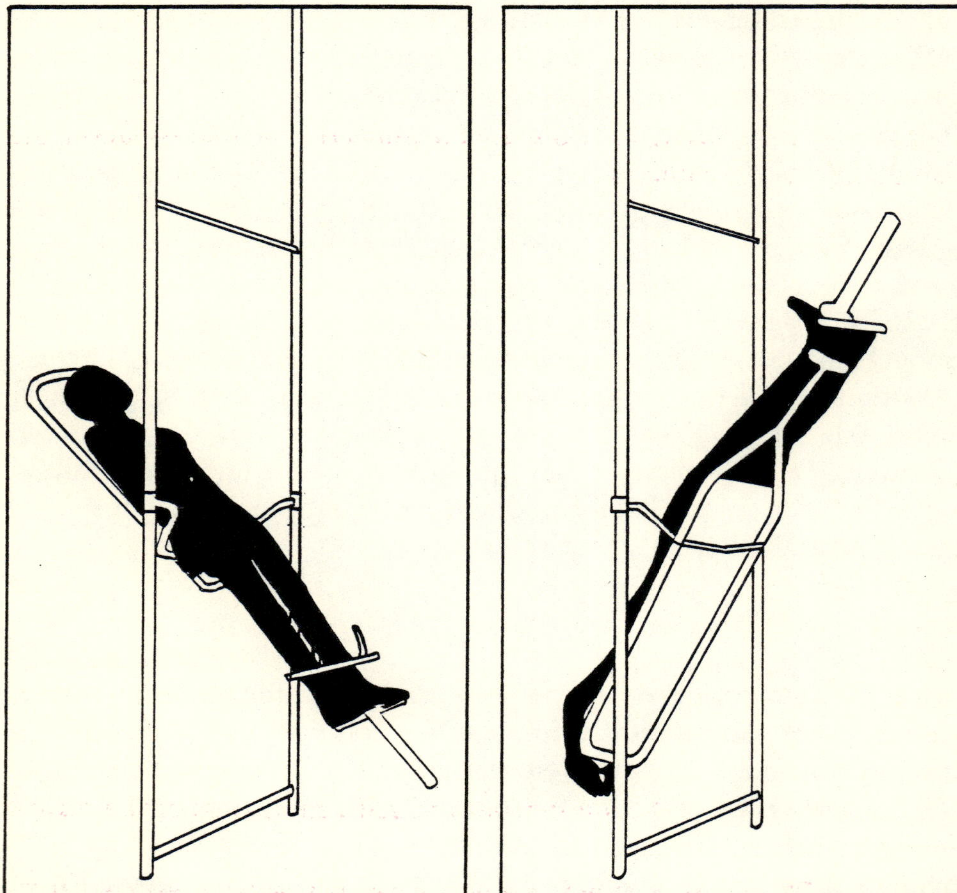

At rest

Upside down

Figure 10b. Backswing

Inverting the body, whatever the apparatus, serves to gently stretch the spine and to release the tension in the neck. In the upside-down position, be it on Iyengar's trapeze or on the backswing, the pull of gravity plus the weight of the head (10 to 14 pounds) no longer bears down upon the neck and shoulders but provides gentle stretching instead; it is a form of passive traction. Lying on a slant board is a gentler alternative to the fully inverted position which is achieved with a backswing machine.

SWIMMING (breaststroke excepted) is recommended by all health care providers. Dr. D. Fardon prefers the elementary side-arm backstroke, because it provides good shoulder and upper back exercise and yet, puts little stress on the neck. The late Dr. C. Lowman, founder of the Orthopaedic Hospital in Los Angeles, frequently prescribed the back stroke accompanied by the frog kick for his patients. Dr. J. Travell warns against the crawl stroke, because it can put too much stress upon the sternocleidomastoid muscle.

What about jogging or running? Dr. J. Travell prefers the INDIAN LOPE instead. Its forward leaning stance greatly improves one's walking posture and its bounding gait slightly exaggerates the weight shift from one foot to the other. Dr. R. Jackson prescribes isometric exercises and considers walking with a book on the top of the head as the best form of exercise.

The strength of the hand grip and the fine mobility of the fingers may be found impaired after the accident. The health care provider can test the strength of the hand grip by measuring it with an instrument especially designed for that purpose. Exercise with THERAPY PUTTY and the HAND HELPER (Meddev Corporation) can help strengthen the hand grip and can also improve the fine mobility of the fingers (Figures 10c and 10d) (see RESOURCES chapter).

The Chinese have for centuries recommended that a "HEALTH BALL" be rotated with the fingers in the palm of each hand. This motion puts pressure on a sensitive acupuncture point inside the palm which is located on the heart meridian. The stimulation of this point is supposed to be helpful in cases of shoulder periarthritis, numbness of the hands, cervical syndrome and it is also claimed that it is beneficial to brain function. Any ball that is about 2½ inches in diameter may be used for this purpose (see RESOURCES chapter).

BEHAVIOR MODIFICATION

Avoidance of activity which would aggravate the injury is as important as treatment and exercises. Postures, movements and activities which can trigger a recurrence of whiplash symptoms should be avoided. Whiplash patients must modify their behavior, avoiding all forms of spectator's stance (a posture of constant alertness in which the head is thrust forward in front of the shoulders), because it brings on neck muscle strain.

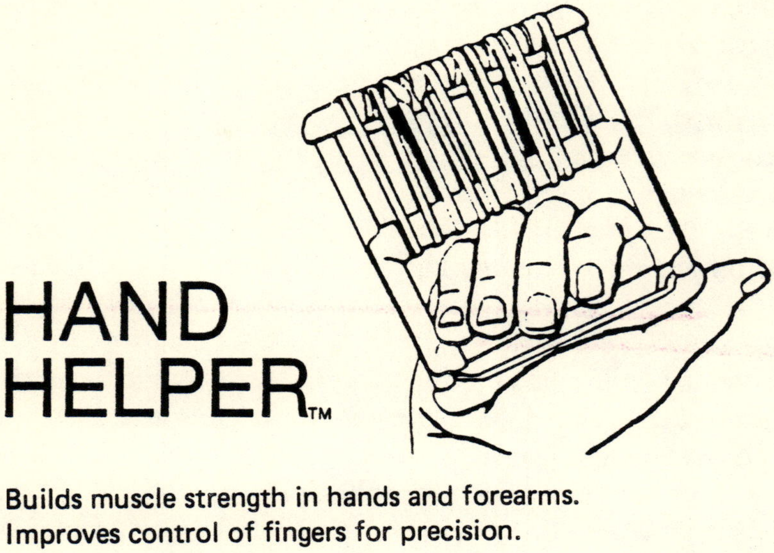

Figure 10c. Therapeutic aids

The following are also to be carefully avoided: watching television, reading or sleeping, while lying on the stomach; long sustained effort that requires stretching the neck as in reaching and looking upward; turning the torso while bending at the waist and heavy lifting. The greatest stress on the neck and the shoulders is caused by the effort made

Figure 10d. Therapeutic aids

in lifting objects that are held out away from the body; whenever lifting an object, the whiplash patient should hold it as close to the body as possible.

Power steering and an adjustable steering wheel should be considered a must; speed bumps or pot holes are to be avoided or negotiated at greatly reduced driving speed. Also beware of shampoo basins in beauty salons; a hairdresser can put the neck under considerable stress while shampooing the hair, by forcing the neck backward, the edge of the basin acting as a fulcrum.

Eyeglasses with bi-focal lenses cause the user to throw the head back, thus subjecting the neck to extra stress. Dr. J. Travell points out that prolonged reading, while wearing glasses, can also place extra strain upon neck muscles. To avoid such strain, Dr. J. Travell recommends that either eyeglass frames be tilted downward to bring the lower rim against the cheek; or that "card-playing" corrective lenses which have a more adequate focal length, be selected.

In summary, the patient should learn and practice proper posture, maintain mobility, avoid acute prolonged extension backward of the neck and limit prolonged hyperflexion forward. Lengthy, uninterrupted automobile drives should therefore be avoided. At the theater, balcony seats are preferable to orchestra seats. Dr. R. Jackson's patients receive a booklet illustrating the proper posture to assume for common activities; it is excerpted from her book, *The Cervical Syndrome.* (See Appendix for reprint of Dr. R. Jackson's booklet: *Instructions for Patients with Neck Disorders.*)

When symptoms of discomfort and pain recur, as they often do, they are usually triggered by one of the "to be avoided" activities or postures listed above, and another round of treatment may then be necessary.

Dr. D. Fardon recommends a self-help posture for one-sided neck pain which can bring quick relief. Lie down on the side, a bolster under the pain-free side of the neck, so that the head falls over the bolster, and the ear on the non-painful side approaches the shoulder. Remain in that position for between 5 and 15 minutes.

Trigger Points

Between the twelfth and the eighteenth weeks a marked improvement should be noticed by the great majority of whiplash patients. There may, however, be some stubborn residual pain in "trigger points." Bonnie

Prudden defines a trigger point as neuromuscular memory of trauma, usually found in muscles; in Dr. R. Cailliet's words, "pain is the cry of a nerve deprived of its normal blood supply." It will most often occur near the insertion of the muscle into the bone. It is an area of vasoconstriction where the blood flow is being impeded. The pain resulting from a trigger point can induce muscle spasm, which in turn may begin a pain-spasm-pain-spasm cycle.

Dr. J. Travell points out that people with long, supple necks are more prone to develop sore trigger-points than people with short, stocky necks. To alleviate this kind of pain, patients can seek the treatments pioneered by Dr. J. Travell; one is the STRETCH & SPRAY technique: the sore muscles are fully stretched while being sprayed with a vapocoolant of Fluori-Methane (TM). The other is the INJECT & STRETCH method: a procaine solution is injected into the painful muscle at the same time it is stretched.

Other options may be: Bonnie Prudden's Myotherapy, John Thie's Touch for Health, acupuncture, or Dr. R. Lawrence's OSTEOMASSAGE (see RESOURCES chapter). There is a point at the inner tip of the shoulder blade, two inches away from the spine, where neck and shoulder muscles attach to the bone. This osteopoint can be quite painful following a whiplash injury and can flare up when a tense posture is kept for a long period of time. The massage of this osteopoint is done in small circular motions and is supposed to help restore the function of the parasympathetic nervous system.

The timing of the healing process is approximately as follows: muscles generally heal within a few weeks. Dr. R. Cloward anticipates a minimum of 3 months for the healing of torn ligaments. Dr. J. Bland warns that torn invertebral disks take much longer (pain in the shoulder blade and numbness in the hands may be caused by a torn intervertebral disk). A plateau is reached after six months. Approximately 10% of whiplash victims will, however, continue to have severe symptoms long after the accident. When headaches, tingling of the fingers, visual or auditory disturbances or dizziness are still present more than 6 months after the injury, an objective neurological loss and a possible chronic disability may be involved. Some structural changes may also occur, such as loss of lordosis (the normal forward curve of the neck). Calcium deposits may also form later on the edges of some vertebrae; these osteophytes or "spurs" represent an effort at stabilization of the five-point balance system of the vertebrae, according to Dr. M. Abel. Spurs result in a decreased range of motion and arthrosis (i.e., joint degeneration without inflammation) which, in turn, will impinge on some cervical nerve roots and irritate them.

Acupuncture

Dr. L. Wensel considers acupuncture the safest and most effective treatment for whiplash residuals. Dr. Wensel bases her opinion upon her own private practice and upon a study that was conducted by the Washington Acupuncture Center in St. Petersburg, Florida, from 1973 to 1976. A total of 76 cases suffering from whiplash residuals received between 6 and 16 acupuncture treatments. The results were significant improvement in 52 cases and no improvement for 5 cases. The remainder showed modest improvement. Dr. L. Wensel includes in the term whiplash residuals: pain in the neck, headaches, osteoarthritis of the cervical spine and cervical pathology. These chronic conditions may in turn put pressure upon cervical nerves thereby causing painful muscle spasms, stiffness and limitation of movement; numbness and tingling in the arms and hands may also be present.

In order to obtain optimum benefits from acupuncture, Dr. L. Wensel recommends 2 grams of Vitamin C and 100 mg of Pantothenic Acid be taken daily, and that extra iron and copper be avoided. Dr. P. Chan advocates acupressure self-help therapy on some of the same meridian points that are listed by Dr. L. Wensel for acupuncture treatment.

Dr. B. Brown remarks that for most physicians, active treatment of symptoms without evident neurologic or bone cause seems futile and such symptoms are frequently dismissed as a psychogenic illness. Thus the alternative therapies described above fulfill a need which standard medicine generally has not recognized.

CONSUMER, BEWARE

The following treatment methods should be very carefully evaluated; there is either the possibility of mistreatment arising from misdiagnosis or they are considered controversial:

1. BIOFEEDBACK is now one of the treatment modalities available for tinnitus (ringing in the ears); however, it is not effective when the condition is caused by a concussion.

2. WRIST SURGERY. There are two separate syndromes that pro-

duce somewhat similar symptoms (weakness and numbness in the hands as well as tingling in the fingers) but which have different causes: the CARPAL TUNNEL SYNDROME (caused by the entrapment of one of the nerves in the wrist) and RADICULITIS (cervical nerve root irritation). The first one can be relieved by wrist surgery; the second cannot.

This cervical nerve root irritation may be due, in Dr. H. Kabat's opinion, to an herniated cervical disc between the 6th and the 7th neck vertebrae. That disc is quite vulnerable to a whiplash injury because it is located at the junction of a relatively mobile part of the spine (the neck) and a rather static part (the upper back).

Dr. J. Travell, on the other hand, states that numbness and tingling in the fingers, weak hand grip and swelling of the hands are neither caused by the carpal tunnel syndrome nor by radiculopathy. She instead attributes the condition to the 3 scalene muscles which she has nicknamed the "entrappers." Attached to the cervical vertebrae #3 through #6, they flex the neck and keep the cervical spine stabilized. They can also entrap the brachial plexus and the subclavian veins: this will cause the symptoms mentioned above by interfering with normal blood flow.

3. URETHRA DILATION: a NEUROGENIC BLADDER occasionally follows a whiplash injury; the bladder does not empty normally because the delicate balance between the sympathetic nervous system and the parasympathetic nervous system (see Chapter 3: THE NECK) has been disturbed. Urethra dilation is sometimes recommended for that condition, even though it is now considered an obsolete procedure with unwelcome side effects.

These three conditions: ringing in the ears, tingling of the fingers and numbness of the hands, and a neurogenic bladder are susceptible of showing a marked improvement, after a course of acupuncture treatments, according to Dr. L. Wensel.

4. The PSYCHOTHERAPY of choice, according to Dr. R. Jackson, is for the health care provider to explain the physiological basis for the psychological changes the patient is undergoing. This will put the patient's mind at ease and provide an incentive to focus on the regimen prescribed for a prompt recovery. Psychotherapy at this juncture is rarely appropriate. The patients' psychological state will, as a rule, progressively improve as they recover from their physical injuries.

Chapter 6

PREVENTION

What can be done to prevent or at least minimize a whiplash injury? Since muscular development seems to protect against the severity of whiplash injuries to a degree, strong muscular short necks are not at risk to the same extent as long slender necks. Women whose slender necks make them particularly vulnerable to whiplash trauma, might strengthen their neck muscles by lifting weights, as a preventive measure against neck injury. Young football players are encouraged to work at bar bells regularly by the American Football Coaches Association, for the same purpose: a weak neck would make a player overly susceptible to neck injury when exposed to the common stresses of football.

CAR DESIGN

The element of surprise also plays a role. If the occupant of the rear-ended vehicle is forewarned that a collision is imminent, and braces against the impact, the whiplash injury may be less severe than if the impact takes the occupant completely by surprise. However, the occupant of the car which is struck from behind usually has no forewarning that a collision is imminent. Further, as hyperextension and hyperflexion of the neck occur within the first quarter second after the impact, a last moment warning may provide insufficient time for muscle reflexes to come into play.

The design of the car seat can protect the neck to a degree; individual front seats are preferable to bench-type seating. The seat back should be at least 28 inches high and well padded to absorb the impact. Experts concur that a properly designed head support can minimize most whiplash injuries. The head support acts as a head stop in a rear-end collision and prevents the head from being thrown back too far upon impact.

If the head support is high enough to reach the top of the ears (at least ten inches above the seat back itself), the shoulders and the head will accelerate at approximately the same speed, in a rear-end collision. It is the difference in velocity between the supported upper torso and the unsupported head that compounds the whiplash injury (Figure 11). The most expensive cars do not necessarily have the best designed seat backs. Some head supports are poorly designed to fulfill the protective function they are expected to serve. Many are not quite high enough, while others are insufficiently padded. Dr. M. Hohl points out that only 20% of the adjustable head supports were found positioned at a level adequate to be effective in preventing injury. That is most unfortunate indeed; when head supports became mandatory in 1969, it was estimated that half of the whiplash injuries could be prevented by proper head supports. Dr. M. Hohl states that the high seat back performs well, but has other drawbacks; presumably one of the drawbacks Dr. Hohl refers to is impaired visibility.

A few years after head supports had become required standard equipment, a study of insurance claims for whiplash injuries was carried out in Southern California. Its purpose was to see whether there had been a great decrease in the number of neck injury claims against insurance companies, once head supports became the norm. The study did show a marked decrease in the number of neck injury claims lodged against insurance companies, but Dr. Brian O'Neill and his co-researchers were disappointed that the decrease was not larger.

They suspected that these disappointing results may have been due in part to the fact that the great majority of adjustable head supports are not positioned properly. Television advertising focuses on the speed capabilities of new cars, not on the proper positioning of their adjustable head supports. Owners' manuals should explain how to properly position head supports, but so far, very few do. The kind of head supports which have their metal supports exposed (result from an) "inept design error" according to Dr. B. O'Neill and his co-researchers. On the other hand, SAAB's adjustable high seat back meets with their approval because it provides good protection while not restricting rear vision. Severy, the well known automobile safety expert, is quoted as saying that "head restraints should be an integral part of the vehicle, preferably requiring no adjustment, if they are to provide the most consistent and effective protection against rear-end collision injuries."

SAAB, the Swedish automobile manufacturer, does remind its customers that the head rest cushion should bolster the back of the head, not the neck, in order to offer effective protection against whiplash injuries. It also advises that a seat back which is slightly reclined, instead of being

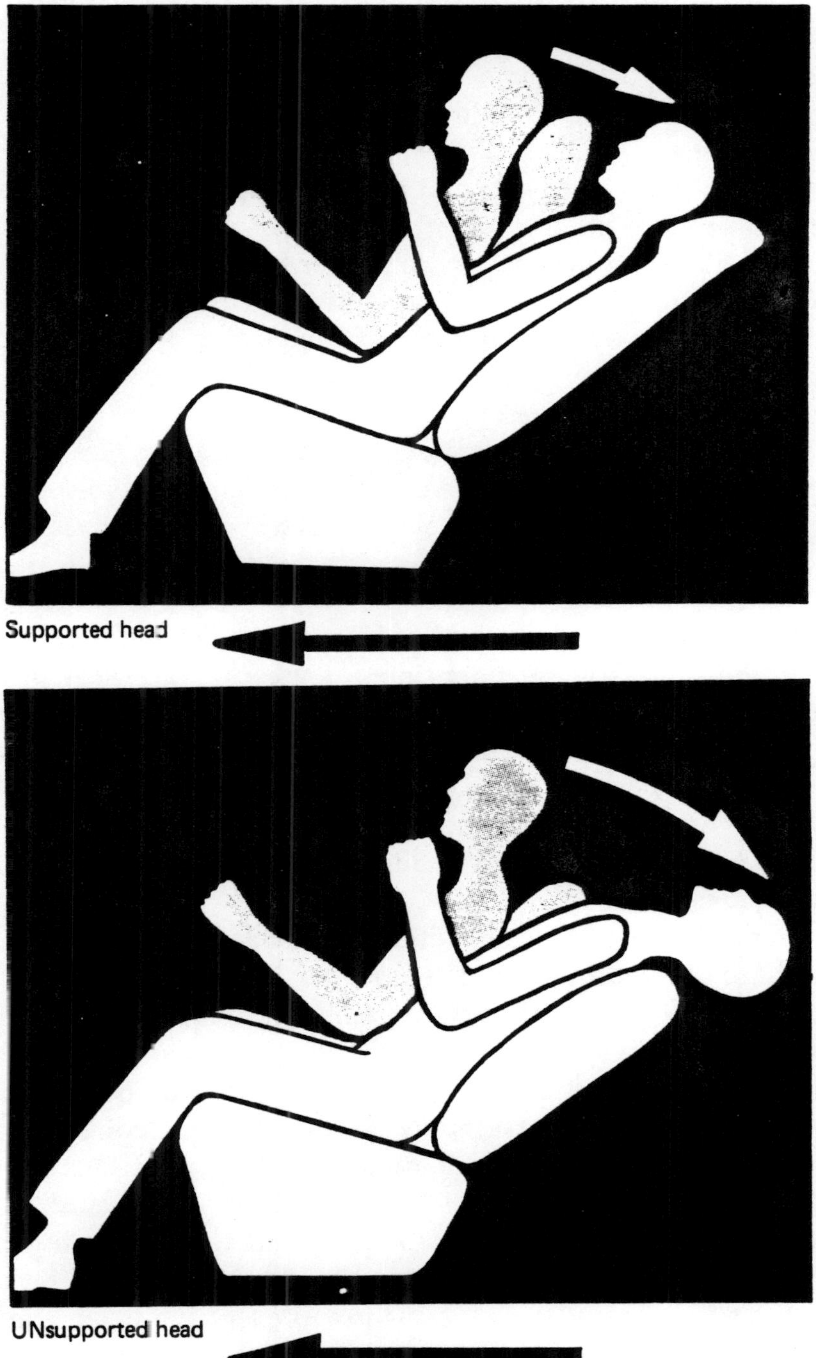

Figure 11. Recommended automobile seat back

upright, will improve the passenger's chances of avoiding a neck injury in a rear-end collision (*Changing Times*, March 1987, p. 123).

When head supports became mandatory some twenty years ago, it was estimated that this feature would cut whiplash injuries in half. Was this optimism premature? Dr. R. Bailey, for one, has reservations as to the effectiveness of high seat backs and of head supports; he indicates they may in fact produce other types of head and neck injuries and expects that the possibility of neck injury in rear-end collisions will be with us for the foreseeable future. Some automotive executives are also dubious about the effectiveness of head supports; one was quoted as saying that he had not found "one guy whose life was saved or who even avoided a sprained neck with a headrest."

When shopping for a new car, the consumer should pay close attention to the design of the car seats. There is still some way to go before all car seats look like the bucket seat model that was recommended years ago by the Liberty Mutual Insurance Company and endorsed by Dr. R. Jackson. In the opinion of Drs. M. Panjabi, T. Wetzel and A. White, a firm seatback is safer, because the motion of the head and the loads causing injury to the spine are dependent upon seatback stiffness. A firm seat also results in lesser shear stresses. It would be very helpful if consumer magazines, which provide car ratings every year, included an evaluation of the protective merits of car seat designs. At present, *Consumer Reports* in its yearly auto issue, only evaluates car seat support for the lower back; it does not deal with the capability of car seats to protect the upper back and the neck.

Although, as Dr. J. Travell points out, automobile seats have been among those which do least to help one maintain correct posture, there seems to be a new trend in the making. Chrysler, for one, is advertising a lumbar-contoured seat as an extra. Porsche also offers an adjustable orthopedic seat, albeit at a very steep price. Special contoured orthopedic seats manufactured in Germany are available to replace stock car seats: besides providing adjustable lumbar support, the RECARO (TM) seats also have special headrests. They cost about $500, including head support. Reportedly, some doctors recommend them to their patients with back problems, as replacements for standard equipment.

Seat belts and shoulder harnesses can prevent many injuries, but contrary to a very common misconception they do not prevent whiplash injuries. What seat belts and shoulder harnesses do is prevent the occupants from being thrown out of the vehicle, and further reduce the extent of injuries by restraining the occupant from striking the interior surfaces of the vehicle when a collision occurs. In addition, a driver using a seat belt is better able to maintain control of the vehicle in an emergency.

Some car owners feel they are safer in a big, heavy car; indeed, according to *Changing Times*, November, 1983, it has been found that small cars are on the receiving end of 18% more rear-end collisions than full size cars.

The *Injury Fact Book* never addresses whiplash injuries specifically but it confirms that the size of the respective vehicles can play a very important role in determining the severity of the injuries inflicted upon the passengers of the rear-ended vehicle, if the latter is smaller than the colliding vehicle. As they point out, "most injuries from vehicle collisions result when mechanical energy is conveyed to people in amounts or at rates that exceed their injury thresholds." Hence, "vehicle size is a major determinant of the severity of occupant injuries in a crash, as occupants of smaller vehicles in two-vehicle collisions are at a major disadvantage because of the greater forces inflicted on the smaller vehicle by the larger one." Occupants of subcompact cars with a wheelbase 96 inches long or less are especially at risk. This represents a frightening trade-off for the sake of gasoline economy, maneuverability and parking convenience.

What are U.S. automobile manufacturers doing to improve seat design and to protect car occupants, insofar as possible, against whiplash injuries? Automotive engineers presently use the 50th Percentile Man, an anthropomorphic test dummy, as a standard for testing new car designs. The male dummy is 35.7 inches high and the female dummy 30.9 inches high when seated erect. Starting in 1991, the National Highway Traffic Safety Administration will require auto manufacturers to use the Hybrid III Dummy instead of the one currently used. General Motors designed the model and petitioned the NHTSA for approval. They believe this dummy is a significant improvement over the present model. As previously noted, women's necks are far more susceptible to whiplash injuries than those of men. To what extent any of these dummies accurately reflect the vulnerability of most women's necks to whiplash injuries remains unclear.

The Big Three auto manufacturers also have advisory committees that cater to the Women's Automotive Market. They are concerned with cosmetic touches such as sun-visor mirrors, seats that don't snag fur coats and flooring that won't scuff high heel shoes. Their concern has even gone to the extreme of having male committee members simulate women's fingernails by attaching paper-clips to their fingertips, the better to test the accessibility of knobs, dials and handles. Their paper-clip test apparently resulted in trunk latches which are easier to operate, according to *Changing Times,* (July 1987, p. 82).

Since 1986, the National Highway Traffic Safety Administration has required an additional brake light mounted in the middle of the rear window, as standard equipment on all new cars. A driver following a car equipped with such an extra brake light can see this braking signal faster because it is in the middle of his or her field of vision. In addition, this signal helps reduce the reaction time of the following driver. This is an inexpensive feature which can easily be retrofitted on cars sold prior to 1986. (Blinking lights or lights that spell words out should be avoided, as they are prohibited by federal standards.) The Federal Traffic Safety Administration expects that the introduction of this additional brake light will mean 900,000 fewer rear-end accidents and 40,000 fewer injuries per year (*Los Angeles Times,* May 30, 1987, II, 4).

In 1973 a study was carried out in San Francisco on the effectiveness of the CYBERLITE (TM) signal system in yellow cabs. It showed that the CYBERLITE center-mounted brake light improved the visibility of signals in lead vehicles in a line of traffic and that rear-end collisions were cut by half.

Dr. I. MacNab has pointed out that whenever passengers were facing the back of the vehicle instead of the front, at the time of the rear-end collision, although they did experience uncontrolled flexion of the neck, none of them ever complained of neck pain. In his view, this confirms that it is the acceleration/extension phase of the accident which traumatizes the neck by snapping it back far beyond the physiologically permitted limit.

The National Highway Traffic Safety Administration is now providing consumers with comparative head injury ratings to help them make automobile purchasing decisions. The data are thus far limited to crash tests in head-on collisions. Nothing of the kind is available yet for rear-end collisions.

DRIVER EDUCATION

One simple prevention measure that is completely overlooked is the bus riding rule: "No unnecessary conversation with the driver allowed."

This rule needs to be extended to all vehicle passengers. Many rear-end collisions are reported to result from a momentary distraction on the part of the driver who is engaged in an absorbing conversation or even argument with a passenger. Both Dr. J. Janes and Dr. H. Hoosmand stress that the most important preventive measure would seem to be the education of the careless driver who is the cause of the rear-end collision.

Futurists predict that in twenty-five years, sonar shields will automatically brake a car, whenever it comes too close to another. Perhaps this will put an effective end to rear end collisions and whiplash injuries.

Heidi J. Christiansen, CMA
500 Beech Street
Chaska, MN 55318

Chapter 7

COMPENSATION FOR WHIPLASH INJURIES

Although the driver and owner of the rear-ending vehicle may be legally liable for the injuries incurred by the whiplash patient, the victim or victim's attorney must usually negotiate a financial settlement with the company insuring the liable parties. Special damages—that is, loss of income, and the cost of medical care and car repairs—can usually be recovered without difficulty once itemized and submitted to the insurance carrier. But general damages—which include compensation for pain and suffering—are much more difficult to recover.

Most state laws allow compensation for pain and suffering as an element of general damages in auto accident injury cases. But when damages are sought for whiplash injuries, those against whom the claim is made are often very skeptical that the victim's pain and suffering has been real, and of such degree that the victim is entitled to financial compensation.

Moreover, a victim with serious injuries may be reluctant to agressively pursue adequate compensation, perhaps feeling it to be self-indulgent to barter pain and suffering for money, or having no stomach for the confrontation and advocacy involved in negotiation, or fearing the social suspicion and stigma which may be generated by demands for an adequate financial settlement.

However, the whiplash victim should take stock of several compelling facts: by law, the driver and owner of the rear-ending vehicle bear responsibility for any harm caused by the negligent operation of their vehicle; the negligence of the driver of the rear-ending vehicle caused the victim's injury; the symptoms and disabilities which are caused by a whiplash injury usually subside, only to sometimes recur again and again, years after the injury was incurred; adequate compensation can help pay for treatment and services the victim may later need to cope with chronic whiplash residuals.

MEDICAL PROFESSION'S ATTITUDE

There will probably continue to be stiff resistance to the payment of adequate compensation to whiplash victims for their pain and suffering, as long as it remains difficult to establish, through objective testing, the source, extent, severity and duration of a whiplash victim's pain and distress. The tests presently available all have severe limitations: either a test is not considered sufficiently reliable (for example, conventional x-rays do not show soft tissue injury per se), or a test is too costly and therefore rarely used.

The lack of dependable testing thus makes it difficult for the whiplash victim to obtain and present evidence to prove the source and severity of the pain and disability which accompanies whiplash injuries; the development of more reliable testing will place the victim in a better position to obtain a reasonable financial settlement.

General damages (including pain and suffering) are damages for injuries which cannot be readily equated with a precise sum of money. The dollar value of general damages is the sum which the negotiating parties determine is reasonable compensation. Even if valid, dependable, and generally accepted testing could be employed, setting adequate compensation for past, present and future distress, and for potential future medical costs and disability, will continue to generate dispute, because it will never be possible to forecast an injury's future course and costs with precision.

In negotiating compensation for whiplash injuries, because the whiplash syndrome includes disparate symptoms, it is often especially difficult to establish that the injuries were incurred in the rear-end accident and were not present before that accident.

In one case, a patient who complained of an atonic bladder (a bladder in which the sphincter fails to function properly) was told by the examining urologist that the condition was a consequence of giving birth to her child 25 years earlier. Nor did the urologist modify his diagnosis when told that the patient had never experienced bladder problems until immediately after the whiplash injury. Was the urologist unaware that such bladder malfunction may result if the trauma of the rear-end collision has disturbed the parasympathetic nervous system?

Medical personnel readily administer tests specially designed to spot malingerers (such tests are beyond the scope of this book); but many medical care providers are reluctant to certify that specific injuries, malfunctions and accompanying distress were caused by the whiplash accident.

Most are loath to become involved in the litigation process and, as previously noted, medical care providers are frequently unsupportive of the patient's efforts to obtain financial compensation for whiplash injuries. Patients' pain and distress are often summarily dismissed with the admonition to relax and take it easy, or with the suggestion they consult a psychiatrist. They are also sometimes urged to settle their claims for damages quickly in the mistaken belief that the patients' symptoms will magically disappear, once a financial settlement is reached.

Whiplash victims often find they are suspected of malingering for financial gain not only by medical personnel, insurance adjusters, and rear-ending drivers, but even by their employers, co-workers, families and friends. Doubt that the symptoms described by the victim are real and as painful and disabling as represented by the patient are probably impossible to dispel completely, since a financial motive does exist to establish the severity of the injury and symptoms.

It has been reported that some medical personnel go so far as to withhold treatment until after the insurance claim has been settled. Presumably only if the patient continues to complain after settlement, is the validity of the complaint established. Hurriedly presented claims generally result in poor settlements because adequate medical documentation of the injury is only possible after treatment is well underway and the diagnosis is more certain. It should not be necessary for the whiplash patient to sacrifice a reasonable financial settlement in order to obtain needed treatment.

Drs. J. Janes and H. Hooshmand saw 10,000 patients with neck pain at the Mayo Clinic, between 1956 and 1963. They reported that "approximately 80% of the patients lose their symptoms within a year from the time of the injury," but 20% of their patients were left with chronic symptoms, such as scar tissue, calcium deposits and degenerative changes in ligaments. It would have been irresponsible to keep these patients waiting for treatment until their claims had been settled. The extensive studies of Drs. Janes and Hooshmand led them to conclude that not all patients with neck pain are neurotic, and that settlement of claims does not relieve all complaints as has been asserted.

Drs. C. Schutt and F. Dohan, in their statistical study of whiplash injuries in women, pointed out that their data did not support the opinion that prolonged symptoms and disability are commonly due to litigation neurosis or malingering; in about 75% of all cases, symptoms continued for more than six months, irrespective of whether there was litigation pending; in only one case out of their 76 case samples did they suspect malingering. Drs. S. Norris and I. Watt also found that "litigation per se had little influence on symptoms."

INSURANCE COMPANIES' POSITION

Insurance companies are usually eager to settle whiplash injury claims as quickly as possible, and for as little as possible. The number of claims for injuries arising out of rear-end accidents in the United States each year has been estimated at about 1,000,000 by Dr. B. O'Neill and his co-researchers; considering the volume of claims, it is not surprising that expediting settlements becomes a high priority for insurance companies, particularly since the elements which enter into the total cost of settlement become more expensive the longer treatment and its documentation continue.

Rather than campaigning for more stringent accident prevention measures and improved vehicle safety design as a means of reducing the amount which they spend to resolve whiplash injury claims, the insurance companies have been making an effort to reduce the cost of settlements, by tagging whiplash injuries as largely fraudulent and by denying whiplash injuries are disabling. They claim they are losing money due to the excessive amounts paid to settle claims and have been campaigning for legislation which would deny most whiplash victims monetary recovery for pain and suffering.

In California, for instance, insurance companies utilized the state election initiative to sponsor three measures on the Fall, 1988 ballot. It is estimated the insurance industry spent 60 million dollars on its unsuccessful campaign to have its 1988 California initiatives passed by the electorate.

The avowed purpose of the insurance companies was to reduce car insurance rates for the average motorist, and return auto insurance to profitability. Two of the insurance company initiatives incorporated "no-fault" provisions, which would have reduced premiums by closely circumscribing the types of injuries for which auto accident victims could recover general damages.

Under the no-fault provisions persons injured in vehicular accidents would have been reimbursed for "special damages," but only in instances of "serious and permanent injury" would "general damages" (which include pain and suffering) have been recoverable.

Moreover, the no-fault provisions would have severely restricted access to lawyers for victims who had incurred whiplash injuries, and would have left many victims to represent themselves in negotiations with insurance companies at the very time when, because of the disabling effects of the injury, they would be least able to do so effectively. Jeffrey O'Connell, a law professor at the University of Virginia and a long time advocate of no-fault insurance, wanted to eliminate what he terms shin-kicking litigation for non-cash losses; those claims, in his opinion, "often amount to exaggerated whiplash claims and the like."

One of the 1988 California ballot initiatives supported by the insurance industry which would have restricted recovery to special damages for most whiplash victims was sponsored by a group which called itself, "Consumers for Lower Insurance Rates"; a prominent caption in their campaign literature admonished the voter to, "Stop the fraud which occurs, when someone yells whiplash and sues for megabucks" thus declaring, in effect, that whiplash victims never have legitimate claims.

Until the Fall, 1988 California election, it was not possible under California law to require the insurance companies to open their financial records to the public and there was no governmental rate setting authority for the industry. However, a modestly funded public interest group calling itself the **"Voter Revolt to Cut Insurance Rates"** sponsored an initiative which gained the endorsement of Ralph Nader, and was passed by the electorate; it provides for the election of an insurance commisioner who will have authority to set insurance rates, and requires the insurance companies to open their books for public examination. Perhaps we will soon know whether in fact the insurance companies are losing money on car insurance policies.

The process of recovering damages for one's injuries is adversarial in nature, and therefore the whiplash victim should keep a diary from the first day following the collision, recording symptoms, medical tests, appointments with doctors and treatments from physiotherapists, time missed from work, and sick leave used. A carefully kept diary can be invaluable in documenting a claim for damages.

Because of the widespread notion that many whiplash complaints are fraudulent, it is best that the victim not submit to any medical examination arranged by the liable parties or their insurance carriers, unless accompanied by an observant witness who can attest to the scope of the examination, its duration, the tests administered, and to the questions asked by the doctor.

The whiplash victim should seriously consider arranging for a representative to negotiate and handle all communications with the representatives of the liable persons or their insurance carriers. If the liable persons are not insured, recovery may be possible under the uninsured motorist provisions of the whiplash victim's own insurance policy.

The central questions involved in deciding upon the sum required to provide adequate compensation for whiplash injuries are these:

> Will whiplash residuals continue to restrict the victim's activities? Hinder his or her career?
>
> Will the victim be required to hire help to perform tasks which the victim previously performed?
>
> Will the victim be required to seek out health care treatment which may not be covered by health insurance?
>
> Is the victim likely to eventually develop chronic disability from the whiplash injury?

As an example of the persistence and significance of whiplash injury residuals, the pianist, Byron Janis, now in his late fifties, incurred a whiplash injury some 25 years ago; he has been forced to limit his piano playing to sixty concerts a year, because of chronic shoulder problems stemming from that injury. (*Los Angeles Times,* September 30, 1984, "Calendar," pp. 50–51).

The potential for future problems from whiplash residuals is seldom given proper weight in settlement negotiations; if it were, settlements would be more substantial than they generally are at present.

Chapter 8

CONCLUSION

Rooted in misinformation and ignorance, there are many commonly accepted fallacies regarding whiplash injuries which, in the public interest and in the interest of the whiplash patient, should be finally put to rest.

COMMON FALLACIES

Fallacy No. 1. **"There cannot be anything wrong with your neck; nothing shows on the x-rays."** X-rays can only show bone injury or vertebral subluxation; they do not show injury to soft tissues. There are now other tests available, which are reliable, even though they are seldom used. Why not take advantage of thermography, CAT-scans or of magnetic resonance imaging to help refine the diagnosis? Cranial osteopaths, with their trained "thinking" fingers, are able to validate the whiplash patient's complaints through palpation of the skull bones and of the cervical vertebrae. So can the majority of other "hands-on" practitioners.

Fallacy No. 2. **"Your neck could not have been injured, because there was no direct impact upon your neck."** A direct impact does not need to take place for a whiplash injury to occur. What causes a whiplash injury, that is an injury to the neck and the hindbrain, is the sudden acceleration/deceleration triggered by the rear-end collision. This, in turn, subjects the neck to brutal hyperextension/hyperflexion, far beyond its normal range of motion. Whenever the whiplash injury includes a "contrecoup" injury, there is additional trauma to the cranial nerves and brain blood vessels, as the soft brain tissues are jostled against the bony skull. The skull no longer acts as a shell protecting the brain but as an instrument contributing to the injury.

Occasionally people will complain of symptoms quite similar to those of whiplash patients, after going on fun rides in amusement parks. Rollercoasters, for instance, depend on sudden acceleration and deceleration for thrills; they may cause whiplash-like symptoms.

Fallacy No. 3. **"Rest and time plus some muscle relaxants and tranquilizers will take care of a whiplash patient's distress."** It is true indeed that time and rest do help. However, without adequate physiotherapy, whiplash patients run the risk of having a chronic problem with a sore, stiff neck. Physiotherapy will help them regain some degree of pain-free mobility and will prepare them for the proper exercise regimen that they will later have to follow. The value of muscle relaxants and tranquilizers is often more than offset by their side effects. Sports medicine has now refined a regimen of cold and hot packs, ultrasound, massage, traction and manipulation that is available from orthopedic specialists, osteopaths, chiropractors and physiotherapists. Whiplash patients should expect the same level of optimum care which athletes receive. Why settle for less? To limit treatment of whiplash injuries to tranquilizers and home rest borders on malpractice.

Fallacy No. 4. **"All those complaints are psychosomatic!"** In this instance, "psychosomatic" is meant to be pejorative and belittling, that is to say, the physical discomfort results from psychological factors only. What psychosomatic actually means is that there is a complex interaction between the body (soma) and the mind (psyche). This close interrelationship works **both** ways. It is completely arbitrary to define it as a **one-way interaction.** There is a very good, organic, reason for the whiplash patient to suffer from anxiety or irritability.

These psychological symptoms usually fade away, as the treatment progresses. Therefore, psychotherapy would be premature to say the least, and may even increase the anxiety of whiplash patients by causing them to wonder whether their physical symptoms are purely mental and without an organic basis. There are homeopathic remedies which can be dramatically effective for symptoms of anxiety and irritability.

Fallacy No. 5. **"Whiplash victims are malingering for monetary gain."** The complaints of whiplash patients are suspected of being tainted with an ulterior motive. There are no statistical studies to support those suspicions. Military personnel, even though they have no legal recourse against the government and nothing to gain financially, also suffer from whiplash injuries. There are tests which are capable of detecting phony complaints.

Rear-end collisions are not the one and only cause of whiplash trauma. Pediatricians have cautioned parents of late, not to shake their infants. Children can be seriously injured when shaken by an adult. The head of a child is large in relation to the rest of the body while the neck muscles are underdeveloped and weak. Whenever a child is severely shaken by an adult, the head bounces back and forth and the brain is bumped against the inner sides of the skull, injuring the brain tissues, blood vessels and nerves. This can cause permanent brain damage, that is to say, diminished mental capacity, paralysis of the limbs, hemorrhage in the eyes resulting in vision problems and even in blindness.

This "Whiplash Shake Syndrome" is now recognized by pediatricians as a form of child abuse. There was recently a case in which death was attributed to the whiplash shake syndrome. (*Los Angeles Daily Journal,* April 23, 1985, p. 22). The District Attorney's office admitted, however, that: "it is very nearly impossible to sell a jury that shaking is a criminal act or that one could expect it to result in death or great bodily injury," so the charge against the stepfather involved in the death of his four-year old stepson was reduced from murder to involuntary manslaughter. If a 175-pound adult can do that much harm to a child, is it any wonder that a 3,000-pound car can severely injure the occupants of the car it has struck?

Fallacy No. 6. "**Settle your insurance claim right now and your discomfort will disappear overnight!**" This is completely contradicted by the clinical experience of several practitioners who pointed out that there was little if any relationship between patients' settlement of claims and the resolution of their symptoms.

Fallacy No. 7. "**If people wore their seat belts, they would not receive whiplash injuries.**" Seat belts have a great protective feature: in the event of collision, they prevent the wearer from being bumped around against the inside of the car and from being thrown out of the car. But, unfortunately, seat belts do not prevent whiplash injuries.

These misconceptions are quite common. Either the whiplash victims are blamed for their plight or the very existence of their injury is denied. Those fallacies stem first from ignorance of the complex anatomy of the neck and the brain; second from a lack of understanding of the chain-reaction along the cervical spine and upward inside the skull, which is triggered by the rear-end collision. In addition, whiplash injuries do not show clearly to the naked eye.

The neck is quite flexible and has a great range of motion in all directions. These essential qualities become a liability in a rear-end collision; the structure of the neck is not able to withstand unscathed the tremendous forces which are applied. Rear-end collisions are so common that whiplash injuries have become a serious hazard of everyday life.

People are aware in a general way how vulnerable the neck can be.

Everyday speech reflects this awareness quite clearly. For example, a **roughneck** is someone strong enough to stand roughhousing: he does not have to worry about receiving a serious injury. If you **stick your neck out**, you are exposing yourself to danger. If you **get it in the neck**, you are being dealt a serious setback—physically, financially, or socially.

At the beginning of this century some people suffered excruciating backaches after taking a long train ride. Seats were hard and shock absorbers insufficient to cushion the bumps. The "railroad spine" is now a thing of the past. When will the whiplash become a historical curiosity and how can this be achieved?

Chapter 9

EXERCISES

Exercises are an effective and important part of the treatment, as they condition the body to tolerate a reasonable amount of stress. They are done to achieve better posture, increased flexibility, strengthening and relaxation. Unused muscles tend to become weak and to shrink in size. Here again, as in treatment, the key word is **stretch.**

The following exercises are recommended by several experts, with this important warning: **never force the motion in any exercise,** as there might be limited range of motion at first. Proceed gently and slowly. At first, exercises will be done only while lying down.

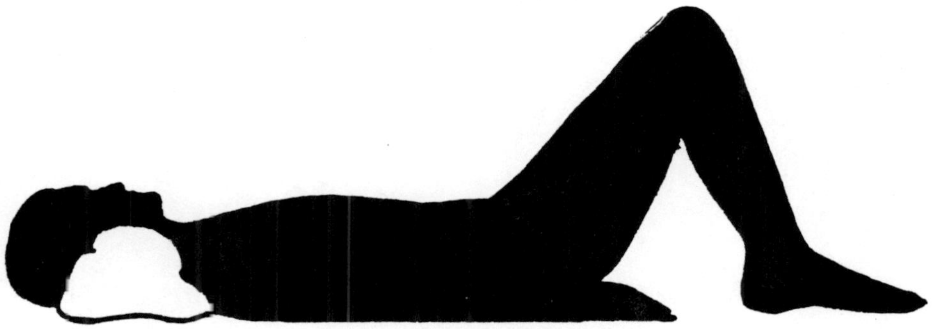

Figure 12a.

1. Lie on your back with knees drawn up and neck supported by a bolster (Figure 12a);
   Take a deep breath, expanding the chest to its limit;
   Exhale slowly;
   Repeat this deep respiratory exercise slowly five times, every morning upon awakening.
2. Lie on your back with knees drawn up and arms at your sides;
   Slowly draw arms back over head and touch hands together;
   Return arms to the sides;
   Repeat slowly three to five times.

3. Lie on your back with knees drawn up;
   Turn your head to the left;
   Return to normal position;
   Now do the same on the right side;
   Repeat exercise three to five times.

Figure 12b.

4. Sit on a hard chair, feet apart on the floor (Figure 12b); (You may also sit on a stool, under a hot shower).
   Let your neck droop;
   Drop your shoulders and your arms;
   Bend down between your knees as far as you can;
   Tighten abdominal muscles and hold;
   Return slowly to an upright position and relax;
   Repeat three to five times.
5. While seated, inhale slowly, shrugging your shoulders as you do so;
   Then relax your shoulders as you exhale.
   Repeat three to five times.

Whenever you are required to sit for a prolonged time and pay careful attention (for instance, while working at a desk, driving a car, or watching a show), the following exercise will be beneficial. It can be done either sitting down or standing under a hot shower.

6. Draw head back and **tuck the chin in** toward the chest (Figure 12c); Take a deep breath;
   a. Raise both shoulders upward as close to the ears as possible and hold, counting to five;
      Relax and let shoulders drop;
   b. Draw shoulders backward as far as possible, counting to five;
      Relax. Repeat three times.
7. "Window in the Sky" is a yoga pose quite helpful in relaxing the neck.
   Lie on your back, your knees drawn up;
   Clasp your hands together **behind your neck** as you inhale;
   Exhale and slowly pull your head up, using your arm muscles; the insides of your palms should be firmly pressing the **sides of your neck;**
   Breathe slowly and deeply through your nose while keeping the head up; keep your eyes closed; press and stretch your neck in this posture for **up to one minute;**
   Bring your elbows together gradually;
   Inhale and slowly lower your head to the floor;
   Relax with your arms at your sides.
8. The "Lion" pose is another yoga posture that is recommended for people who suffer from TMJ (Temporo-Mandibular Joint Dysfunction). It consists of yawning widely.
9. The following exercise is also recommended for good neck posture:
   a. Stand tall and pinch the shoulder blades together;
   b. Hold the head back;
   c. Release shoulder blades.

The following two tension-releasers are not exercises but a form of self-massage which can help relax tense neck and shoulder muscles:

a. Squeeze the right side of the neck with the right hand, moving your hand **up** from the shoulder to where the neck meets the head.
   Repeat on the left side.
b. Put one hand across your chest, grasping the top of the opposite shoulder and squeeze the shoulder muscle.
   Change side.

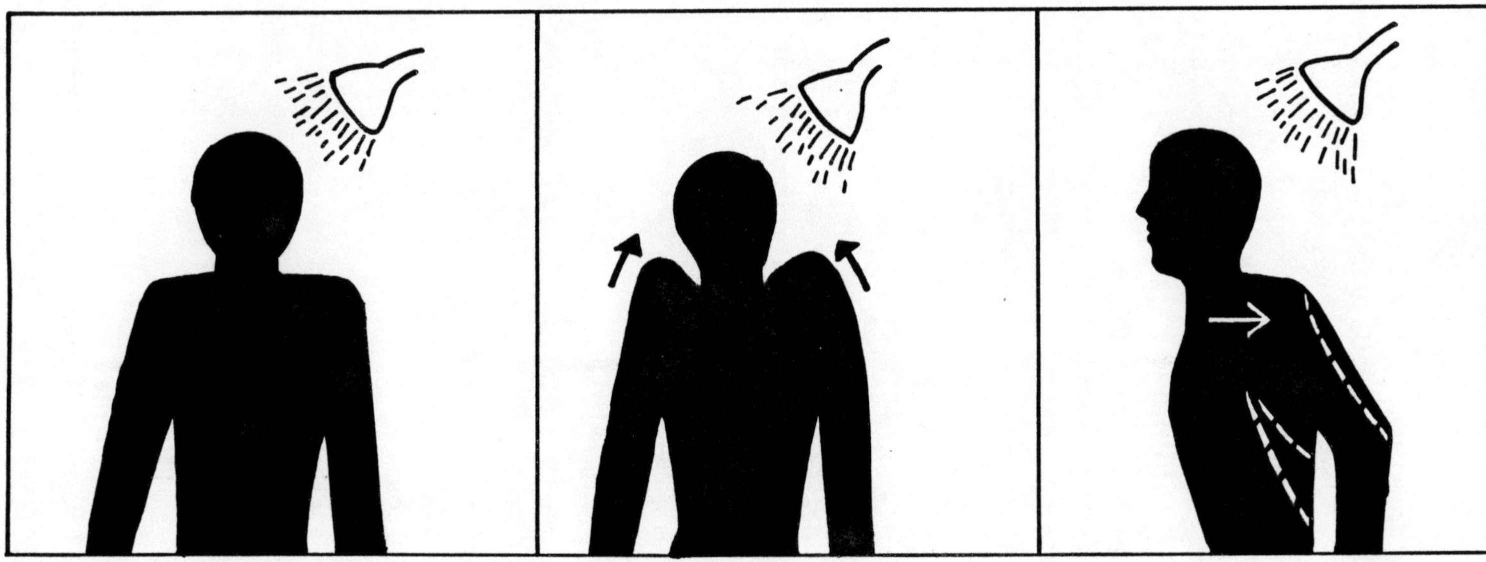

Figure 12c.

Chapter 10

RESOURCES

REFERRAL SOURCES

AMERICAN ASSOCIATION FOR ACUPUNCTURE AND ORIENTAL MEDICINE
5473 66th St. N., St. Petersburg, FL 33709.

AMERICAN MASSAGE THERAPY ASSOCIATION
1130 W. North Lake Shore Ave., Chicago, IL 60626.

AMERICAN NAPRAPATHIC ASSOCIATION
c/o Roy P. Krueger, D.N., 5913 W. Montrose Av., Chicago, IL 60634.

CRANIAL ACADEMY (AMERICAN ACADEMY OF OSTEOPATHY)
1140 W. Eighth St., Meridian, ID 83642.

FELDENKRAIS GUILD
P.O. Box 11145, Main Office, San Francisco, CA 94101.

INSTITUTE FOR PHYSICAL FITNESS AND MYOTHERAPY
Bonnie Prudden, Director, Prospect Hill, Stockbridge, MA 01262.

INTERNATIONAL FOUNDATION FOR HOMEOPATHY
2366 Eastlake, E. #301, Seattle, WA 98102.

NORTH AMERICAN ACADEMY OF MANIPULATIVE MEDICINE
5021 Seminary Road, #125, Alexandria, VA 22311.

OSTEOMASSAGE
Ronald M. Lawrence, M.D., 28240 W. Agoura Rd., CA 91301.

TRADITIONAL ACUPUNCTURE FOUNDATION
American City Bldg #100, Columbia, MD 21044.

ROLF INSTITUTE
P.O. Box 1868, Boulder, CO 80306.

THERAPEUTIC AIDS

CERVIPILLO (TM), a bolster-type pillow designed for comfort while sleeping; Tru-eze Manufacturing Company, P.O. Box 880, Temecula, CA 92390.

CHINESE EXERCISE BALLS, available through *Medical Self-Care* Catalog, 1-Self-Care Center, P.O. Box 130, Mandeville, LA 70448.

GRAVITY GUIDER (TM), Robert M. Martin, M.D., 181 North Hudson Street, Pasadena, CA 91101.

HAND HELPER (TM), Meddev Company, P.O. Box 1352, Los Altos, CA 94022.

THERAPY PUTTY (TM), Fred Sammons, Inc., P.O. Box 32, Brookfield, IL 60513.

THERMOFORE (TM), a heating pad generating moist heat, Battle Creek Equipment Company, 307 West Jackson Street, Battle Creek, MI 49016.

BIBLIOGRAPHY

BOOKS

Abel, Martin S. *Occult Traumatic Lesions of the Cervical and Thoraco-Lumbar Vertebrae.* St. Louis: Green, 1983.

Anderson, Bob. *Stretching.* Bolinas, California: Shelter Pubs., 1980.

Arat, Arsavir. *Neck Sprains as Muscle Injury.* El Paso: Guynes, 1973.

Bailey, Robert W. *Cervical Spine.* Philadelphia: Lea & Febiger, 1974.

Baker, Susan B., Brian O'Neill and Ronald S. Karpf. *Injury Fact Book.* Lexington, MA: Lexington Books, 1984.

Baxt, William G. *Trauma, the first hour.* Norwalk, Connecticut: Appleton-Century-Crofts, 1986.

Blackie, Margery G. *The Patient, not the Cure; the Challenge of Homeopathy.* Santa Barbara: Woodbridge, 1978.

Bland, John H. *Disorders of the Cervical Spine.* Philadelphia: Saunders, 1987.

Bohlman, Henry H. and Enrique Boada. "Fractures and Dislocations of Lower Cervical Spine" *in* Robert W. Bailey, *Cervical Spine* Philadelphia: Lippincott, 1983, Pp. 236.

Cailliet, Rene. *Neck and Arm Pain.* 2nd Ed. Philadelphia: Davis, 1981.

Chan, Pedro. *Acupressure Self-Help Therapy for Neck Pain and Whiplash Injuries.* Monterey Park, CA: Chinese Total Health Center, 1980.

Fardon, David F. *Free Yourself from Neck Pain and Headache.* Englewood Cliffs, NJ: Prentice-Hall, 1983.

Friedmann, Lawrence W. and Lawrence Galton. *Freedom from Backaches.* New York: Pocket Books, 1973.

Goff, C. W., J. H. Aldes and J. O. Alden. *Traumatic Cervical Syndrome and Whiplash.* Philadelphia: Lippincott, 1964.

Gurdjian, E.S. and L.M. Thomas. *Neckache and Backache.* Springfield, IL: Charles C Thomas, 1970.

Head and Neck Injury Criteria: a Consensus Workshop, National Highway Traffic Safety Administration, Washington, DC, March 26–27, 1981.

Hohl, Mason. "Soft Tissue Neck Injuries" *in* Robert W. Bailey, *Cervical Spine.* Philadelphia: Lippincott, 1983. Pp. 282–287.

Ishmael, William K., and Howard B. Shorbe. *Care of the Neck.* Philadelphia: Lippincott, 1966.

Jackson, Ruth. *The Cervical Syndrome.* 4th Ed. Springfield, IL: Charles C Thomas, 1978.

Kabat, Herman. *Low Back and Leg Pain from Herniated Cervical Disc.* St. Louis: Green, 1980.

Kraus, Hans. *Sports Injuries.* Chicago: Playboy Press, 1981.

Kulowski, Jacob. *Crash Injuries.* Springfield, IL: Charles C Thomas, 1960.

Lader, Errol. *T M J; Comprehensive Systems Manual...* New York: Vadare, 1983.

Mac Nab, Ian. "Acceleration-Extension Injuries of the Cervical Spine *in* Rothman, Richard M. and Frederick A. Simeone, *The Spine.* 2nd Ed. Philadelphia: Saunders 1982. Pp. 647–660.

Martin, Robert M. *Gravity Guidance System.* Pasadena, California: Gravity Guidance, 1982.

Neck Owner's Manual. Daly City, CA: PAS Publications, 1981.

Panjabi, Manohar M., Todd Wetzel and Augustus A. White. "Biomechanics of Spinal Injuries" *in* Anthony Sauces, *Mechanisms of Head and Spine Trauma.* Goshen, New York: Aloray, 1986. Pp. 241–253.

Paterson, John K., *Introduction to Medical Manipulation.* Hingham, MA: M T P Press, 1985.

Prudden, Bonnie. *Pain Erasure.* New York: Ballantine, 1980.

Sauces, Anthony and Narayan Yoganandan. "Human Head Injury Tolerance" *in* Anthony Sauces, *Mechanisms of Head and Spine Trauma.* Goshen, New York: Aloray, 1986. Pp. 189.

Sutherland, Adah S. *With Thinking Fingers.* The story of William Sutherland. Kansas City: Cranial Academy, 1962.

Thie, John. *Touch for Health.* Marina del Rey, California: De Vorse, 1973.

Torklus, Detlef Von and Walter Gehle. *Upper Cervical Spine.* New York. Grune and Stratton, 1972.

Travell, Janet G., and David G. Simons. *Myofascial Pain and Dysfunctions; the Trigger Point Manual.* Baltimore: Williams & Wilkins, 1983.

Trimble, M.B. *Post-traumatic Neurosis from Railway Spine to Whiplash.* New York: Wiley, 1981.

Unterharnscheidt, Friedrich. "Pathological and Neuropathologic Findings in Rhesus Monkeys Subjected to −Gx and +Gx Indirect Impact Acceleration" *in* Anthony Sauces, *Mechanisms of Head and Spine Trauma.* Goshen, New York: Aloray, 1986. Pp. 565–566.

Wensel, Louise O. *Acupuncture in Medical Practice.* Reston, Virginia: Reston, 1980.

Wexler, Charles E. *Overview of Liquid Crystal and Electronic Lumbar, Thoracic and Cervical Thermography.* Tarzana, CA: Thermographic Services, 1983.

Wickstrom, Jack and Henry LaRocca. "Head and Neck Injuries from Acceleration/ Deceleration Forces" *in* Daniel Ruge and Leon L. Wiltse, *Spinal Disorders: Diagnosis and Treatment.* Philadelphia: Lea & Febiger, 1977. Pp. 349–355.

Work of our Hands. Meridian, Idaho: Sutherland Cranial Teaching Foundation, American Academy of Osteopathy, 1969.

Yashon, David. *Spinal Injury.* 2nd Ed. East Norwalk, CT: Appleton & Lange, 1986.

NEWSPAPERS AND PERIODICALS

Brown, Burnell R. "Diagnosis and Therapy of Common Myofascial Syndromes," *J A M A,* 1978, Pp. 646–648.

Cloward, Ralph B. "Acute Cervical Spine Injuries," *CIBA Clinical Symposia,* 1980, Pp. 1–32.

Fisher, C. Miller. "Whiplash Amnesia," *Neurology,* 1982, Pp. 667–668.

Fox, Jeffrey L. "Lab Break-in Stirs Animal Welfare Debate," *Science,* 1984, Pp. 1319–1320.

Helliwell, M. et al. "Bilateral Vocal Cord Paralysis due to Whiplash Injury," *British Medical Journal* [Clinical Research ed.] (London), 1984, Pp. 1876–1877.

Hinoki, Manabi. "Vertigo due to Whiplash Injury: a neurotological Approach," *Acta Otolaryngologica.* Suppl. (Stockholm), 1984, Pp. 9–29.

Jacome, D.E. "E E G in Whiplash: a Reappraisal," *Clinical Electroencephalography,* 1987, Pp. 41–45.

Janes, Joseph M. and Hooshang Hooshmand. "Severe Extension-Flexion Injuries of the Cervical Spine," *Mayo Clinic Proceedings,* 1965, Pp. 353–369.

Kelley, James S. "Whiplash Maculopathy," *Archives of Ophthalmology,* 1978, Pp. 834–835.

Liu, Y. Kin, K.B. Chandran, R.G. Heath and F. Unterharnscheidt. "Subcortical E.E.G. Changes in Rhesus Monkeys Following Experimental Hyperextension-Hyperflexion (Whiplash)." *Spine,* 1984, Pp. 329–338.

Norris, S. H. and I. Watt, "Prognosis for Neck Injuries Resulting from Rear-end Vehicle Collisions." *Journal of Bone and Joint Surgery,* 1983, Pp. 608–611.

O'Connell, Jeffrey. "A No-Fault Proposal that Ranks Among the Best, and the Legislature can't gut it." *Los Angeles Times,* November 3, 1988, II: P. 7.

O'Neill, Brian, William Haddon, Jr., Albert B. Kelley and Wayne W. Sorenson. "Automobile Head Restraints: Frequency of Neck Injury Claims in Relation to the Presence of Head Restraints." *American Journal of Public Health,* 1972, Pp. 399–406.

Physical Therapy, 1972, Pp. 1091–1092.

Schutt, Charles H. and F. Curtis Dohan. "Neck Injuries to Women in Auto Accidents; a Metropolitan Plague," *J A M A,* 1968, Pp. 2689–2692.

Shafer, Nathaniel and Robert Shafer. "Traction: its Pros and Cons," *Trauma,* 1985, P. 59.

Torres, Fernando and Sidney K. Shapiro. "The E.E.G. in Whiplash Injury." *Archives of Neurology,* 1961, Pp. 28–35.

"Whiplash Syndrome: Shaking an Infant Can Cause Death," *Los Angeles Times,* April 4, 1982.

Winston, Ken R. "Whiplash and its Relationship to Migraine," *Headache,* 1987, Pp. 452–457.

Yoga Journal, October 1982, P. 34.

APPENDIX[1]

INSTRUCTIONS FOR PATIENTS WITH NECK DISORDERS

Ruth Jackson

Reclining

Always lie or sleep on a hard bed. If the mattress is not quite firm, put a bedboard between the mattress and the springs.

When lying down, sit on the edge of the bed and lie down sideways. When getting up, turn on your side and put your feet on the floor, then push yourself to a sitting position by using your elbow on the side to which you have turned. This will keep your neck and back straight and will prevent any undue strain on your neck.

Lie or sleep on your back or on your side. Never sleep on your abdomen because this keeps your head turned to one side at the maximum position of rotation and puts a constant strain on the neck for long periods of time, or until you change positions.

Do not sleep with one or both arms above your head. This may cut off the circulation of blood to your arm or arms (Fig. 13A).

Sleep on a soft round pillow (a contour pillow), which assures proper positioning of the neck if you lie on your back or on your side (Fig. 13B and C).

Avoid sleeping on hard or thick pillows or sponge rubber pillows. Such pillows raise your head too high and cause your neck to be bent forward, which puts a strain on the structures at the back of your neck (Fig. 13D).

Writing

Do not slump over a desk when you are writing (Fig. 13E). Sit straight and look down at what you are writing and do not keep your head for-

[1]From the book by Ruth Jackson, *The Cervical Syndrome*, Fourth Edition, 1978. Courtesy of Charles C Thomas, Publisher, 2600 South First Street, Springfield, Illinois 62794.

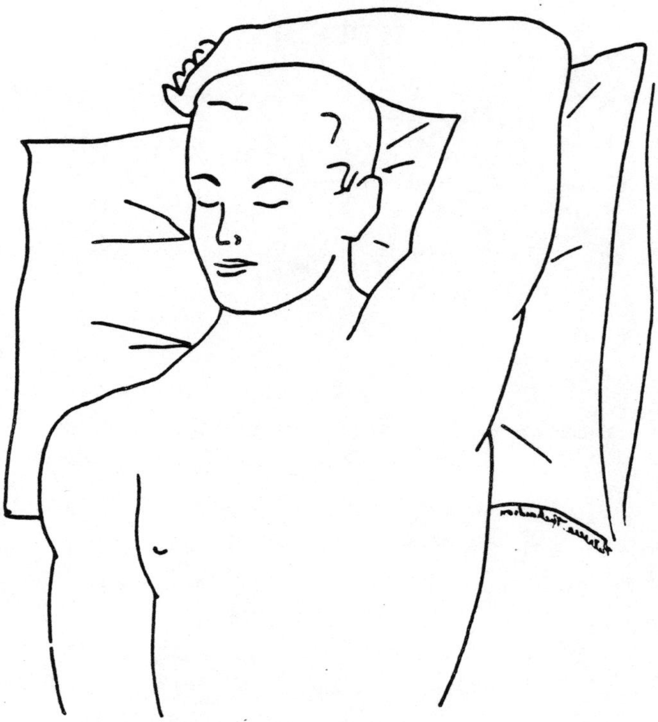

A

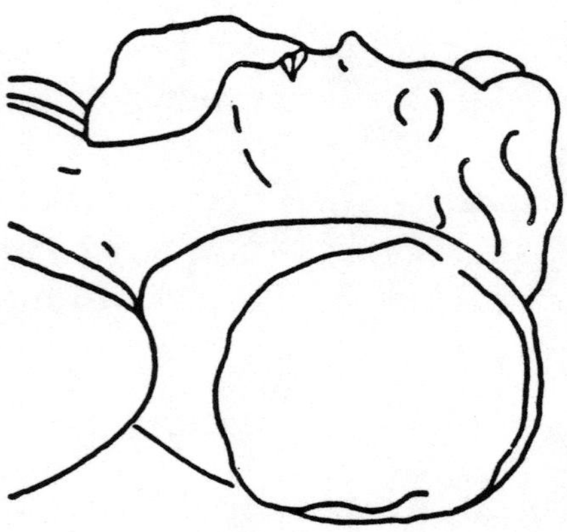

B

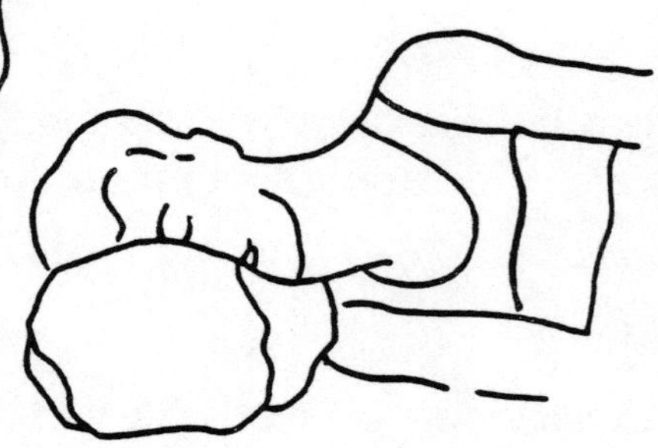

C

Figure 13A through Z′. Illustrated instructions for patients.

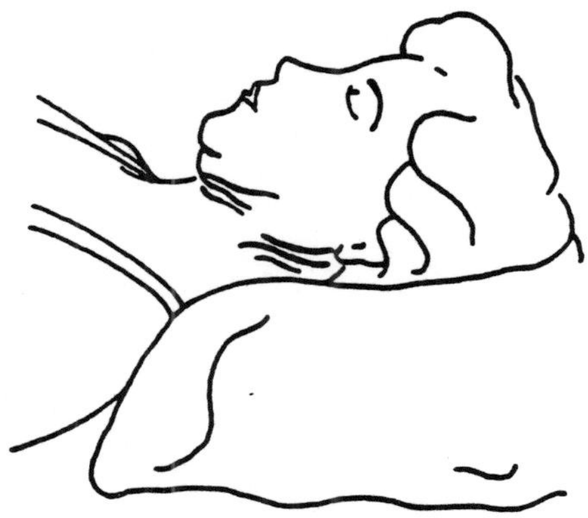

D

Figure 13 Continued

ward or backward. Choose a chair and desk of proper height so that you can see what you are doing without having to hold your head in a forward or backward position. A tilt-top desk is of great advantage (Fig. 13F).

Reading

Do not slump in your chair when you are reading (Fig. 13G). Try to sit erect and keep your reading material as near eye level as possible. A reading stand to hold your book or magazine is of real advantage (Fig. 13H).

Use reading glasses rather than bifocal glasses (Fig. 13I) or have the reading portion of the lenses enlarged or placed at a higher level so that you will not have to put your head backward in order to read (Fig. 13J).

Do not read in bed unless you have the proper backrest. It is difficult to sit erect in bed, and if you try to read, you will soon find yourself slumped over and your head and neck thrust forward (Fig. 13K).

Driving

Keep your car seat as close to the steering wheel as possible. This helps you to sit straight and keeps you from putting your head backward in order to see over the steering wheel and the hood of the car (Fig. 13L and M). Adjustable bucket seats are the most comfortable, and four-way adjustments are desirable.

Armrests at the proper height add to your comfort. Do not lean on the window frame because this makes you sit to the left of the steering wheel. Avoid riding with three people on the seat, especially if this forces or crowds you against the door and away from the steering wheel. Avoid

E

F

Figure 13 Continued

G

H

Figure 13 Continued

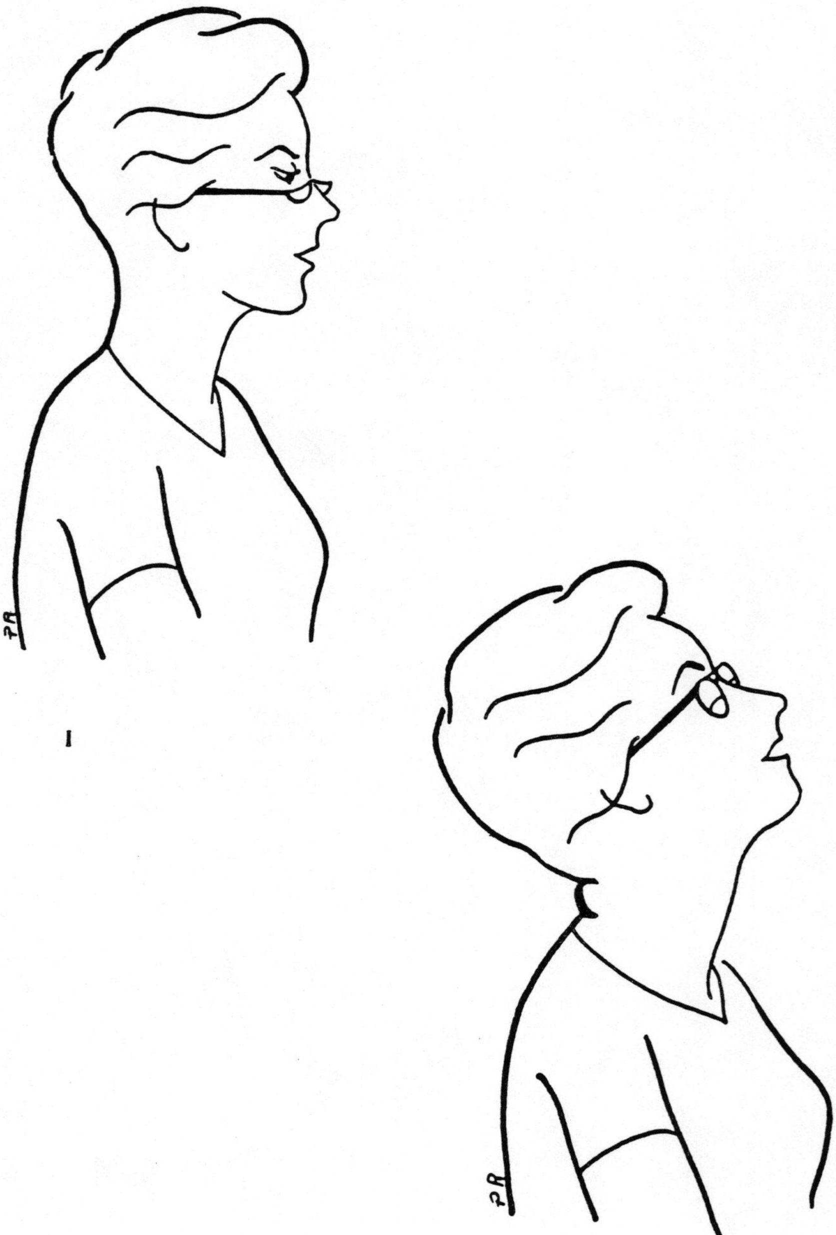

Figure 13 Continued

K

L

Figure 13 Continued

M

Figure 13 Continued

driving for more than an hour at one time. Stop the car, get out, and walk around for a few minutes.

Working

When working, avoid keeping your head held forward, backward, or turned to one side (Fig. 13N, O, P, Q, R, and S). Sit straight, stand straight, and walk straight. Avoid working with your arms above your head. Use a stepstool or a ladder so that whatever work you are doing is near eye level.

Stooping

Learn to squat to pick up things. Do not stoop. When one stoops over, the head and neck go backward automatically (Fig. 13R and U).

N

O

Figure 13 Continued

P

Q

Figure 13 Continued

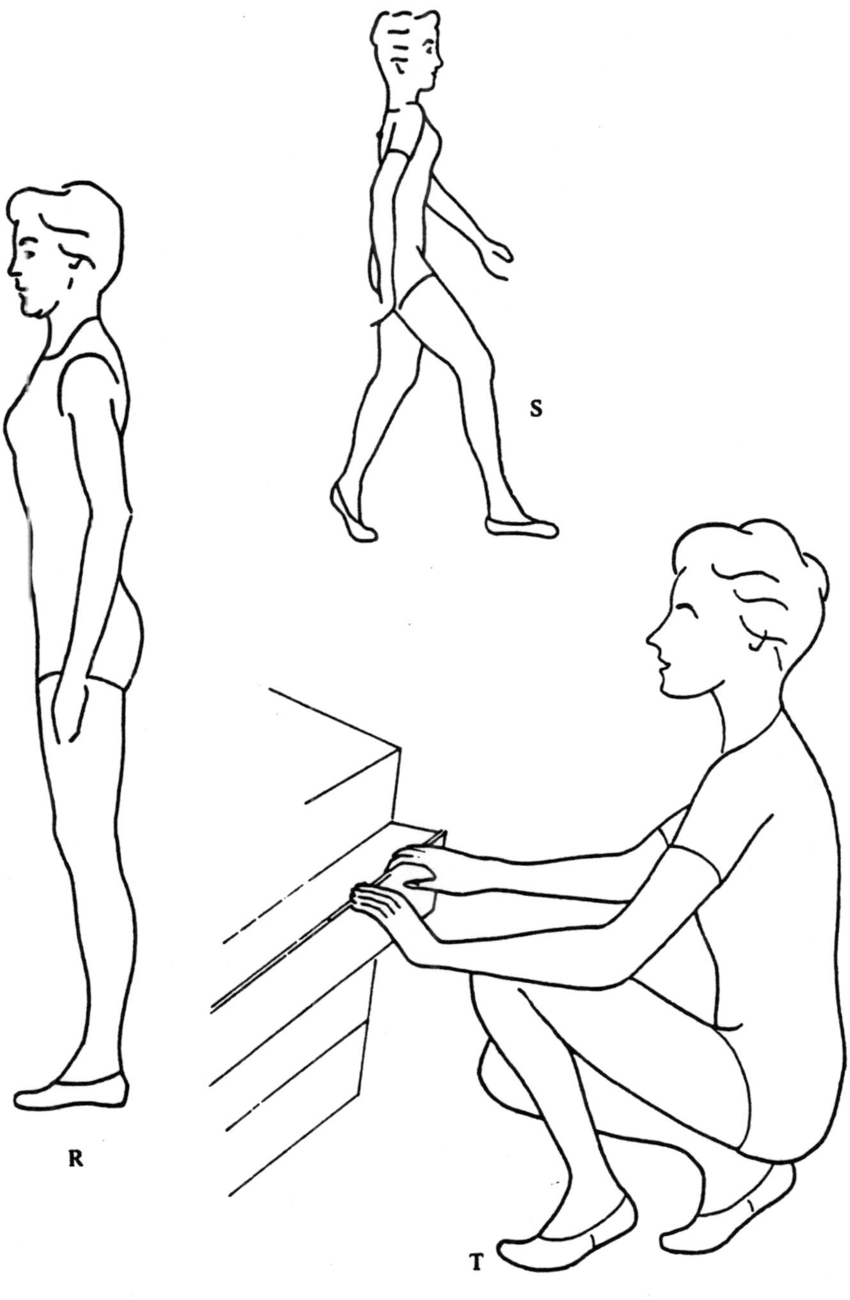

Figure 13 Continued

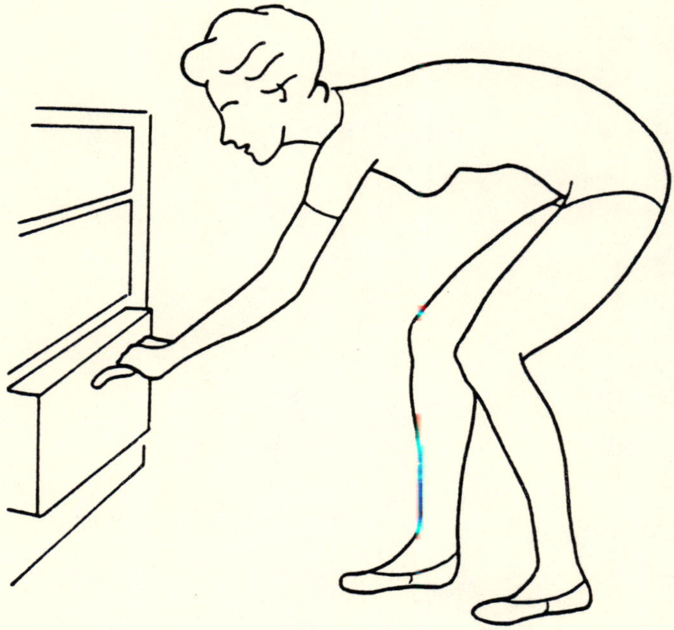

U

Figure 13 Continued

Shaving

Do not put your head backward when shaving under your chin. Avoid stooping over the lavatory to wash your face after you have shaved. Use a washcloth or try conscientiously to keep your chin tucked in if you do stoop (Fig. 13V, W, and X).

Drinking

Avoid drinking from bottles, cans, or narrow-mouthed glasses. Use wide-mouthed glasses or cups so that you will not need to tilt your head backward to drink (Fig. 13Y, Z, and Z′).

The illustrations in Figure 13A through Z′ are visual aids designed to give the patient a better understanding of some of the problems involved, so that he can avoid aggravation of his symptoms while engaging in everyday activities.

Figure 13 Continued

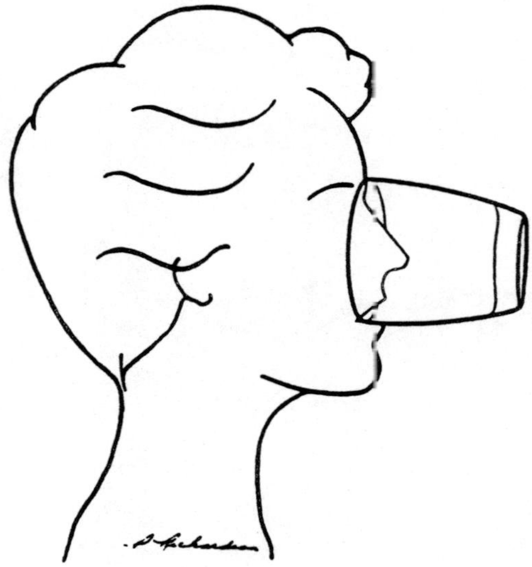

Y

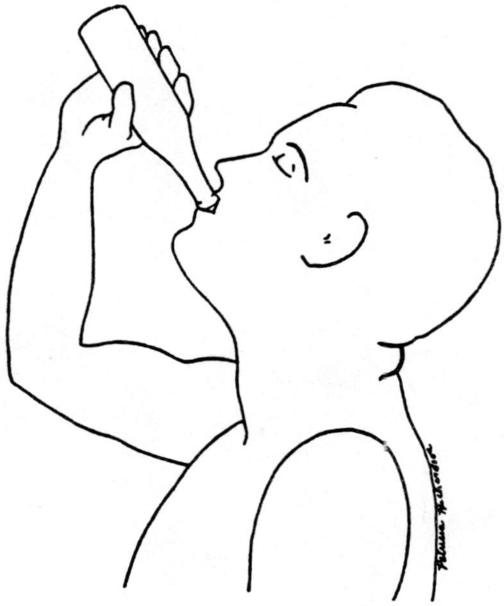

Z

Figure 13 Continued

Z′

Figure 13 Continued

INDEX